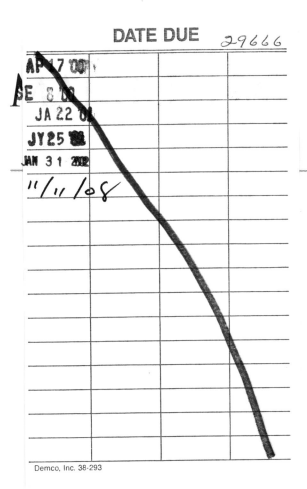

DATE DUE   29666

AP 17 00		
SE 8 00		
JA 22 0		
JY 25		
JAN 31 20		
11/11/08		

Demco, Inc. 38-293

Other Books in the At Issue Series:

MARIJUANA

William Dudley, *Book Editor*

David Bender, *Publisher*
Bruno Leone, *Executive Editor*
Bonnie Szumski, *Editorial Director*
Brenda Stalcup, *Managing Editor*
Scott Barbour, *Senior Editor*

An Opposing Viewpoints® Series

Greenhaven Press, Inc.
San Diego, California

Library of Congress Cataloging-in-Publication Data

Marijuana / William Dudley, book editor.
        p.   cm. — (At issue) (An Opposing viewpoints series)
    Includes bibliographical references and index.
    ISBN 0-7377-0006-8 (pbk. : alk. paper). —
ISBN 0-7377-0007-6 (lib. : alk. paper)
    1. Marijuana. I. Dudley, William, 1964–   . II. Series: At issue
(San Diego, Calif.) III. Series: Opposing viewpoints series
(Unnumbered)
HV5822.M3M37   1999
362.29'5—dc21   98-35006
                                                                                        CIP

© 1999 by Greenhaven Press, Inc., PO Box 289009,
San Diego, CA 92198-9009

Printed in the U.S.A.

Table of Contents

Introduction

Marijuana (also spelled marihuana) is a psychoactive drug made from the dried leaves and flowering parts of the hemp plant. It is one of the most strictly classified illegal drugs in the United States. Under the 1970 Controlled Substances Act, marijuana is listed as a Schedule I substance, which defines it as having "a high potential for abuse" and "no currently accepted medical use." Marijuana is thus classified more severely than morphine and cocaine, which as Schedule II drugs are also banned for general use but can be prescribed by doctors. It is illegal to buy, sell, grow, or possess marijuana in the United States. Marijuana prohibition comprises a large part of the federal government's War on Drugs. Law enforcement officials made 600,000 marijuana-related arrests in 1995—four out of five arrests being for possession alone. Under federal and state laws, many of which were strengthened in the 1980s, people convicted of marijuana offenses face penalties ranging from probation to life imprisonment, plus fines and forfeiture of property. In addition to criminal justice efforts, the federal government, state governments, and local communities spend hundreds of millions of dollars annually on preventative programs such as Drug Abuse Resistance Education (DARE), in which local police officers visit schools to teach young people to refrain from trying marijuana and other drugs.

However, public controversy has been growing over the two assumptions—high abuse potential and no legitimate medical use—that underlie marijuana's status as a Schedule I drug. In turn, disputes over the abuse and medical potential of marijuana have shaped differences of opinion over public policy. Many of those who question one or both of these assumptions about marijuana have advocated a full or partial relaxation of the government's blanket prohibition of the drug, while those who accept these assumptions generally are opposed to any full or partial legalization of marijuana.

Supporters of marijuana's continued prohibition argue that the drug is easily abused and can lead to numerous physical and psychological harms. Short-term health effects of the drug listed in *Marijuana: Facts for Teens*, a publication of the National Institute on Drug Abuse (NIDA), include memory loss, distorted perception, problems with learning and coordination, an increased heart rate, and anxiety attacks. Long-term effects, according to NIDA, include increased risk of lung cancer for chronic marijuana smokers and possible damage to the immune and reproductive systems. In addition, marijuana opponents argue that many users attain a psychological dependence on the "high" that marijuana can create. Such dependence can result in stunted emotional and social maturity as these users lose interest in school, job, and social activities. About 100,000 people each year resort to drug abuse treatment programs to end their marijuana addiction. Marijuana is also viewed by some commentators as a "gateway" drug that can lead to the abuse of other dangerous and illegal substances, including cocaine and heroin.

On the other hand, critics of U.S. marijuana policy argue that the dangers of marijuana have been exaggerated. They contend that many, if not most, users of marijuana suffer no lasting harm, do not move on to other drugs, and do not become addicts. Some surveys on marijuana use in America have shown that nine out of ten people who have tried marijuana have since quit. Researchers working with rats have found that marijuana is a far less addictive substance for the animals than cocaine or heroin. Pro-legalization activist R. Keith Stroup summed up the views of many who oppose marijuana prohibition when he asserted before a congressional committee that "moderate marijuana use is relatively harmless—far less harmful to the user than either tobacco or alcohol."

Whether or not marijuana, as a Schedule I drug, truly has "no currently accepted medical use" is also a matter of public controversy. In November 1996, voters in two states, California and Arizona, passed referenda that legalized marijuana for medical use (these developments and the actions of other states have no impact on marijuana's federal status as an illegal Schedule I drug). Supporters of the California and Arizona initiatives maintain that marijuana is effective in alleviating the symptoms of medical conditions such as AIDS, glaucoma, and multiple sclerosis. Anecdotal evidence of marijuana's efficacy, advocates claim, comes from AIDS patients who have used marijuana to restore appetite and cancer patients who have smoked it to combat nausea caused by chemotherapy treatments—often as a last resort when legally prescribed medicines have failed. Those who contend that marijuana has useful medical purposes call for the federal government to at least reclassify the drug as a Schedule II substance that can be prescribed by doctors. As stated by Lester Grinspoon, a Harvard University psychiatrist, marijuana's continued prohibition as a Schedule I substance "is medically absurd, legally questionable, and morally wrong."

The California and Arizona referenda legalizing medical marijuana were strongly opposed by prominent federal government officials, including the director of the Office of National Drug Control Policy, Barry McCaffrey, who criticized the measures as being "dishonest" and asserted that marijuana "is neither safe or effective" as medicine. Opponents argue that the very concept of medical marijuana is absurd because it is not, like most modern medicines, a synthesized chemical whose composition can be precisely manufactured and controlled. Instead, it is taken from a plant and consists of four hundred chemicals whose exact composition varies with each "dose." Furthermore, they assert, marijuana's claimed medical effectiveness has not been demonstrated by clinical trials. Marijuana's psychoactive properties may make people feel better, contends Robert L. Peterson, a former Michigan drug enforcement official, but that "does not make a drug a medicine." Marijuana opponents maintain that better legal medical alternatives to marijuana exist—including Marinol, a pill available by a physician's prescription that contains THC, the main active ingredient in marijuana. An additional concern voiced by many is that legalizing marijuana for medical purposes would send the wrong message to America's youth. "At a time when our nation is looking for solutions to the problem of teenage drug use," asks Thomas A. Constantine, head of the Drug Enforcement Administration, "how can we justify giving a stamp of approval to an illegal substance which has no legitimate medical use?"

Whether or not marijuana's possible medical advantages outweigh its potential harm is a central question in current debates about this controversial drug. The authors in *At Issue: Marijuana* present various opinions on the benefits and drawbacks of marijuana as well as the public policy measures concerning it.

1

Marijuana Should Be Legalized for Recreational and Medical Purposes

R. Keith Stroup

R. Keith Stroup is founder and executive director of the National Organization for the Reformation of Marijuana Laws (NORML), an organization that advocates the legalization of marijuana.

Marijuana can be harmful when abused, and its use by minors should be discouraged. However, when used responsibly and in moderation, marijuana is far less harmful than tobacco or alcohol. Its continued criminal prohibition by the government is a wasteful and destructive social policy that results in the needless arrests of thousands of otherwise law-abiding citizens. Marijuana should be legalized or decriminalized. At the very least, it should be made available by medical prescription for patients who need it to alleviate suffering.

Editor's Note: The following is taken from testimony delivered on behalf of NORML before the Subcommittee on Crime of the Judiciary Committee, U.S. House of Representatives, on March 6, 1996.

Since 1970, the National Organization for the Reform of Marijuana Laws (NORML) has been a voice for Americans who believe it is both counter-productive and unjust to treat marijuana smokers as criminals. Arresting and jailing otherwise law-abiding citizens who happen to be marijuana smokers serves no legitimate societal purpose. Rather it is an enormous waste of valuable law enforcement resources that should be focused on truly serious crime, and it has a terribly destructive impact on the lives, careers and families of those Americans who are arrested and jailed. We have declared war against a whole segment of our own citizens, without cause. It is time to end marijuana prohibition.

We do not suggest that marijuana is totally harmless or that it can-

Reprinted from R. Keith Stroup's congressional testimony before the Subcommittee on Crime, Committee on the Judiciary, U.S. House of Representatives, March 6, 1996.

not be abused. That is true for all drugs, including those which are legal. We do believe that moderate marijuana use is relatively harmless—far less harmful to the user than either tobacco or alcohol, for example—and that any risk presented by marijuana smoking falls well within the ambit of choice we permit the individual in a free society. Today, far more harm is caused by marijuana prohibition than by marijuana itself.

Recreational marijuana smokers

It's time we put to rest the myth that smoking marijuana is a fringe or deviant activity, engaged in only by those on the margins of American society. In reality, marijuana smoking is extremely common, and marijuana is the recreational drug of choice for millions of mainstream, middle class Americans. According to 1994 National Institute on Drug Abuse (NIDA) data,[1] between 65 and 71 million Americans have smoked marijuana at some time in their lives, and 10 million are current smokers (have smoked as at least once in the last month). In fact, NIDA found that 61% of all illicit drug users report that marijuana is the only drug they have used; this figure rises to 80% if hashish (a marijuana derivative) is included. A national survey of voters found that 34%—one-third of the voting adults in the country—acknowledged having smoked marijuana at some point in their lives.[2] Many successful business and professional leaders, including many state and federal elected officials from both political parties, admit they have smoked marijuana. We should begin to reflect that reality in our state and federal legislation, and stop acting as if otherwise law-abiding marijuana smokers are part of the crime problem. They are not, and it is absurd to continue to spend law enforcement resources arresting them.

Far more harm is caused by marijuana prohibition than by marijuana itself.

Marijuana smokers in this country are no different from their nonsmoking peers, except for their marijuana use.[3] Like most Americans, they are responsible citizens who work hard, raise families, contribute to their communities, and want a safe, crime-free neighborhood in which to live. Because of our marijuana laws, these citizens face criminal arrest and imprisonment solely because they choose to smoke a marijuana cigarette when they relax, instead of drinking alcohol. They simply prefer marijuana over alcohol as their recreational drug of choice. This is a misapplication of the criminal sanction which undermines respect for the law in general and extends government into areas of our private life that are inappropriate.

Responsible marijuana use

At NORML, we believe that marijuana smokers, like those who drink alcohol, have a responsibility to behave appropriately and to assure that their recreational drug use is conducted in a responsible manner. Neither marijuana smoking nor alcohol consumption is ever an excuse for misconduct of any kind, and both smokers and drinkers must be held to the same standard as all Americans.

The NORML Board of Directors in February 1996 issued the following statement entitled *Principles of Responsible Cannabis Use*, which defines the conduct which we believe any responsible marijuana smoker should follow.

I. ADULTS ONLY

Cannabis consumption is for adults only. It is irresponsible to provide cannabis to children.

Many things and activities are suitable for young people, but others absolutely are not. Children do not drive cars, enter into contracts, or marry, and they must not use drugs. As it is unrealistic to demand lifetime abstinence from cars, contracts and marriage, however, it is unrealistic to expect lifetime abstinence from all intoxicants, including alcohol. Rather, our expectation and hope for young people is that they grow up to be responsible adults. Our obligation to them is to demonstrate what that means.

II. NO DRIVING

The responsible cannabis consumer does not operate a motor vehicle or other dangerous machinery impaired by cannabis, nor (like other responsible citizens) impaired by any other substance or condition, including some medicines and fatigue.

Responsible marijuana smokers present no threat or danger to America, and there is no reason to treat them as criminals.

Although cannabis is said by most experts to be safer than alcohol and many prescription drugs with motorists, responsible cannabis consumers never operate motor vehicles in an impaired condition. Public safety demands not only that impaired drivers be taken off the road, but that objective measures of impairment be developed and used, rather than chemical testing.

III. SET AND SETTING

The responsible cannabis user will carefully consider his/her set and setting, regulating use accordingly.

"Set" refers to the consumer's values, attitudes, experience and personality, and "setting" means the consumer's physical and social circumstances. The responsible cannabis consumer will be vigilant as to conditions—time, place, mood, etc. —and does not hesitate to say "no" when those conditions are not conducive to a safe, pleasant and/or productive experience.

IV. RESIST ABUSE

Use of cannabis, to the extent that it impairs health, personal development or achievement, is abuse, to be resisted by responsible cannabis users.

Abuse means harm. Some cannabis use is harmful; most is not. That which is harmful should be discouraged; that which is not need not be.

Wars have been waged in the name of eradicating "drug abuse", but instead of focusing on abuse, enforcement measures have been diluted by targeting all drug use, whether abusive or not. If marijuana abuse is to be targeted, it is essential that clear standards be developed to identify it.

V. RESPECT RIGHTS OF OTHERS

The responsible cannabis user does not violate the rights of others, observes accepted standards of courtesy and public propriety, and respects the preferences of those who wish to avoid cannabis entirely.

No one may violate the rights of others, and no substance use excuses any such violation. Regardless of the legal status of cannabis, responsible users will adhere to emerging tobacco smoking protocols in public and private places.

As these principles indicate, we believe there is a difference between use and abuse, and the government should limit its involvement and concentrate its resources to discourage irresponsible marijuana use. Responsible marijuana use causes no harm to society and should be of no interest to the government in a free society.

The war on marijuana smokers

The "war on drugs" is not really about drugs; if it were, tobacco and alcohol would be your primary targets. They are the most commonly used and abused drugs in America and unquestionably they cause far more harm to the user and to society than does marijuana. Instead, the war on drugs has become a war on marijuana smokers, and in any war there are casualties. According to the latest FBI statistics, in 1994 nearly one-half million (482,000) Americans were arrested on marijuana charges. That is the largest number of marijuana arrests ever made in this country in any single year, and reflects a 67% increase over 1991 (288,000). Eighty four percent (84%) of those arrests were for possession, not sale. Those were real people who were paying taxes, supporting their families, and working hard to make a better life for their children; suddenly they are arrested and jailed and treated as criminals, solely because of the recreational drug they had chosen to use. This is a travesty of justice that causes enormous pain, suffering and financial hardship for millions of American families. It also engenders disrespect for the law and for the criminal justice system overall. Responsible marijuana smokers present no threat or danger to America, and there is no reason to treat them as criminals. As a society we need to find ways to discourage personal conduct of all kinds that is abusive or harmful to others. Responsible marijuana smokers are not the problem and it's time to stop arresting them.

Experience with marijuana decriminalization

Our most comprehensive modern study of marijuana policy was the report of the National Commission on Marijuana and Drug Abuse, Marijuana, A Signal of Misunderstanding (1972).[4] Established by Congress, the Marijuana Commission found that moderate marijuana smoking presents no significant risk to the user or to society, and recommended that the country "decriminalize" minor marijuana offenses; i.e., that penalties be removed for personal use and possession. Following that report, eleven American states adopted modified versions of decriminalization, led by Oregon in 1973. Each of these states retained a modest civil fine for minor marijuana offenses, but eliminated arrest and jail, substituting a citation, similar to a traffic ticket. The advantage of this approach to the marijuana smoker is obvious: the individual is spared the indignity of an arrest and the threat of jail, and avoids a criminal record. But this approach also benefits law enforcement by freeing up police to focus on serious crime.

Nearly one-third of Americans live in states which have now had a 15–20 year real-world experience with marijuana decriminalization, and the experience has been overwhelmingly favorable.[5] Contrary to the fears expressed by some, marijuana usage rates (both the percentage reporting having ever used marijuana, and the frequency of use by those who do smoke) are the same in states that have decriminalized and in states where marijuana smokers are still arrested. Nor has there been any change in attitudes toward marijuana use among young people (high school seniors) in those states. In short, the evidence indicates that we can stop arresting marijuana smokers without harmful consequences.

Time for peace, not war

As a nation, we've talked too long and too loud in the language of war. It's time that we begin to talk of peace. It's time to seek a policy that minimizes the harm associated with marijuana smoking and marijuana prohibition—a policy that distinguishes between use and abuse, and reflects the importance we have always attached in this country to the right of the individual to be free from the overreaching power of government. Most of us would agree the government has no business knowing what books we read, the subject of our telephone conversations, or how we conduct ourselves in the privacy of our bedroom. Similarly, whether we smoke marijuana or drink alcohol to relax is simply not an appropriate area of concern for the government.

Marijuana usage rates . . . are the same in states that have decriminalized [marijuana] and in states where marijuana smokers are still arrested.

The subcommittee is right to be concerned about adolescent drug use of all kinds. We all want our children to grow up safe, healthy and drug free. The data showing an increase in marijuana smoking among adolescents is strong testimony to the failure and ineffectiveness of our drug education programs—including most prominently the Drug Abuse Resistance Education (DARE) program. NORML would be pleased to work with this subcommittee and others to develop more effective programs to discourage adolescent marijuana smoking, and to instill in children an understanding that neither marijuana smoking, tobacco smoking or alcohol drinking is appropriate behavior for minors. NORML's involvement in such a campaign might enhance the campaign's credibility with young people.

But we don't arrest responsible adult alcohol drinkers because we want adolescents to avoid alcohol, and neither can we justify arresting responsible adult marijuana smokers to protect our underage children from marijuana smoking. By stubbornly defining all marijuana smoking as criminal, including that which involves adults smoking in the privacy of their home, we are wasting police and prosecutorial resources, clogging courts, filling costly and scarce jail and prison space, and needlessly wrecking the lives and careers of genuinely good citizens. It's time we ended marijuana prohibition and stopped arresting and jailing hundreds of thousands of average Americans whose only "crime" is that they smoke marijuana. This is a tragic and senseless war against our own citizens; it must be ended.

Medical marijuana

The final point I would like to make to the subcommittee is that marijuana should immediately be made available by prescription to the tens of thousands of seriously ill Americans who need marijuana to alleviate pain and suffering. Of all the negative consequences of marijuana prohibition, none is as tragic as the denial of medicinal marijuana to those who need it.

Because of the importance we place on the need for medical marijuana, we had asked if we might have Harvard Professor Lester Grinspoon, an international authority on medical marijuana, present our testimony here today, but were told by the committee that would not be possible. Dr. Grinspoon, a psychiatrist, is a professor at the Harvard Medical School and a well published author in the field of drugs and drug policy. He has authored more than 140 articles in scientific journals and twelve books, including *Marihuana Reconsidered* (Harvard University Press, 1971); *The Speed Culture: Amphetamine Use and Abuse in America* (Harvard University Press, 1975); *Cocaine: A Drug and Its Social Evolution* (Basic Books, 1976); *Psychedelic Drugs Reconsidered* (Basic Books, 1979); and most relevant for this discussion, *Marihuana, The Forbidden Medicine* (Yale University Press, 1993), which has been translated into nine languages. Dr. Grinspoon is available should this committee elect to hear from him at some point.

The question of permitting medical marijuana must be separated from the question of decriminalizing or legalizing marijuana for recreation use. These are separate issues and they must be judged on their own merits. The country has reached a consensus on the former, even as we remain divided on the latter.

The question of permitting medical marijuana must be separated from the question of . . . legalizing marijuana for recreation use.

On the question of whether seriously ill patients should have legal access to marijuana to relieve pain and suffering, 85%[6] of the American public already support this change. Many of them (22%) have had a family member or friend sick with cancer, AIDS, multiple sclerosis, glaucoma or some other potentially devastating disease, who has had to risk arrest and jail to obtain marijuana to alleviate the side effects of cancer chemotherapy, overcome the AIDS wasting syndrome, or treat other life threatening or serious illnesses. Basic compassion and common sense demand that we allow these citizens to use whatever medication is most effective, subject to the supervision of a physician.

Although more research is needed, it is clear from available studies and rapidly accumulating anecdotal evidence that marijuana is a valuable therapeutic in the treatment of a number of serious ailments[7] and that it is both less toxic and costly than the conventional medicines for which it may be substituted. In many cases it is more effective than the commercially available drugs it replaces. Groups such as the American Public Health Association[8] and the Federation of American Scientists[9] have endorsed the medical use of marijuana.

Marijuana is an effective means of overcoming the nausea and vomiting associated with cancer chemotherapy, and the nausea and appetite loss in the wasting syndrome of AIDS. It is useful for various spastic conditions including multiple sclerosis, paraplegia, and quadriplegia. It also lowers intraocular pressure in people who suffer from open-angle glaucoma. For some people with epilepsy it is the only anticonvulsant that works. For centuries, it has been used as an analgesic and is considered by many to be the best approach to migraine. It is also useful to some patients for the symptomatic treatment of depression, menstrual cramps, asthma and pruritus.

Many seriously ill patients in this country are already using marijuana to reduce their pain and suffering, even though it means they and their families must risk arrest. Informal buyers' clubs, which supply marijuana to the seriously ill, have been formed in many cities. Some of these clubs are small and clandestine; a few, such as the one in San Francisco,[10] operate openly and serve several thousand clients on a regular basis. Despite these heroic efforts, the underground emergency distribution system reaches only a small proportion of the tens of thousands of patients who could benefit from legal marijuana.

NORML first raised this issue in 1972 in an administrative petition asking that marijuana be moved from schedule I to schedule II of the federal Controlled Substances Act, so that it could be prescribed as a medicine. After 16 years of legal battles and appeals, in 1988, the DEA's own administrative law judge, Judge Francis Young, found that "marijuana has been accepted as capable of relieving distress of great numbers of very ill people, and doing so with safety under medical supervision. It would be unreasonable, arbitrary and capricious for DEA to continue to stand between those sufferers and the benefits of this substance in light of the evidence in this record."[11] Judge Young recommended "that the Administrator transfer marijuana from Schedule I to Schedule II, to make it available as a legal medicine". The DEA Administrator overruled Judge Young, and the Court of Appeals allowed that decision to stand, denying medical marijuana to seriously ill patients. Congress must act to correct this injustice.

Notes

1. National Institute on Drug Abuse, *National Household Survey on Drug Abuse: Population Estimates—1994* (Department of Health and Human Services, Public Health Service, Bethesda, MD, 1995).

2. ACLU National Survey of Voters' Opinions on the Use and Legalization of Marijuana for Medical Purposes (March 31-April 5, 1995).

3. National Commission on Marijuana and Drug Abuse, *Marijuana, A Signal of Misunderstanding* (New York: The New American Library, Inc., 1972).

4. Id.

5. Single E.W., "The Impact of Marijuana Decriminalization: An Update," (*Journal of Public Health Policy*, Vol. 10, P. 456-66, 1989); Johnston L., O'-Malley P., and Bachman J., *Marijuana Decriminalization: The Impact on Youth, 1975–80* (Monitoring the Future, Occasional Paper Series #13); Maloff D., "A Review of the Effects of the Decriminalization of Marijuana," (*Contemporary Drug Problems*, Fall 1981).

6. Ibid, at 2.

7. Grinspoon L., Bakalar J., *Marihuana, the Forbidden Medicine* (Yale University Press, New Haven, Conn., 1993); Grinspoon L., Bakalar J., "Marihuana as a Medicine: A Plea for Reconsideration," (*JAMA*, June 21, 1995, Vol. 273, No. 23); The American Public Health Association, *Resolution 9513, Access to Therapeutic Marijuana/Cannabis* (APHA Public Policy Statements, Washington, DC, November 1995); Federation of American Scientists, *Medical Use of Whole Cannabis* (Washington, DC, 1994); National Task Force on Cannabis, *The Health and Psychological Consequences of Cannabis Use* (Australian Government Publishing Service, Canberra, Australia, 1994); Institute of Medicine, National Academy of Sciences, *Marijuana and Health, A Report of a Study by a Committee of the Institute of Medicine* (National Academy Press, Washington, DC, 1982).

8. The American Public Health Association, *Resolution 9513, Access to Therapeutic Marijuana/Cannabis* (APHA Public Policy Statements, Washington, DC, 1995).

9. Federation of American Scientists, *Medical Use of Whole Cannabis* (Washington, DC, 1994).

10. Goldberg C., "Marijuana Club Helps Those In Pain," (N.Y. Times, February 25, 1996).

11. *In the Matter of Marijuana Rescheduling Petition, Docket 86-22, Opinion, Recommended Ruling, Finding of Fact, Conclusions of Law, and Decision of Administrative Law Judge*, September 6, 1988 (Drug Enforcement Agency, Washington, DC, 1988).

2

Marijuana Can Destroy the Lives of Teens

Per Ola d'Aulaire and Emily d'Aulaire

Per Ola d'Aulaire and Emily d'Aulaire are contributing editors to Reader's Digest *magazine.*

A profile of a Chicago teenager reveals the devastating effects marijuana had on her school performance, her family life, and her health, culminating in her hospitalization for heart problems after taking marijuana and cocaine. Marijuana affects the body and brain in numerous ways, and can destroy both the health and lives of teens who use it and become addicted.

When Heather Brooks entered high school in 1991, her guidance counselor pegged her as someone with high potential. In her first semester, she earned top grades. She participated in many extracurricular activities. A student of classical piano, Heather filled her family's suburban Chicago home with Chopin and Beethoven.

During her freshman year, 14-year-old Heather made friends with some older kids, and her life took a sudden turn. One evening while she was with them in a neighborhood park, a tall, good-looking junior named Justin handed her a marijuana cigarette. "Take a drag," he urged. "It'll mellow you out."

At first Heather held off. She'd always disapproved of drugs. But Justin reassured her. "It's not a drug," he said. "It's only pot."

Heather decided to give it a try. "Okay," she conceded. "Just one puff."

With instructions from her friends, she pulled the sweet-smelling smoke into her lungs and held it there until she thought she'd burst. Then came more puffs. As she blew out the wispy remnants of smoke, she felt dizzy—and euphoric. "Give me another drag," she begged, tugging on Justin's arm.

Marijuana contains around 60 compounds called cannabinoids. The most psychoactive of these is delta-9-tetrahydrocannabinol (THC). Differences among plants cause the potency of marijuana to vary widely. But as a result of selective breeding, some of the marijuana smoked today can contain ten to 20 times more THC than there was in the pot smoked in the 1960s and early '70s. More than 400 other chemicals are also found in the plant. Many of their effects are still unknown.

When Heather pulled the smoke into her lungs that evening, the THC molecules slipped through tissue-paper-thin air sacs in her lungs and entered her bloodstream. Within minutes a hefty dose of THC was headed for Heather's brain.

A biological barrier in the brain admits the oxygen, nutrients, hormones and sugar it needs while blocking out unnecessary, sometimes harmful, compounds. Certain psychoactive drugs, however, can pierce this shield. Fat-soluble, the THC and other cannabinoids dissolve in the brain's cellular membranes, which are composed of fat molecules; then, like wet bars of soap, they slip through the barrier.

After a few more drags on the joint, Heather felt a deepening glow of contentment. Time slowed to a crawl. Colors and sounds seemed more intense. *Wow!* she thought. *This stuff is fantastic!*

Her high lasted four hours.

The THC and other cannabinoids would remain in her body for weeks. The molecules dissolve not only in the brain but also in the liver, lungs, kidneys, testes and ovaries.

Unlike alcohol and other water-soluble drugs that are eliminated from the body fairly rapidly, cannabinoids slowly leach from the fat and re-enter the bloodstream before finally being purged via the urine.

Heather couldn't wait for the next invitation from her new friends. Because she'd taken the big step and smoked a joint, she felt a strong bond with them. She was confident someone would bring more pot to share.

She wasn't disappointed. The next weekend, when Justin offered her a joint, Heather took it eagerly. *Why do adults get so bent out of shape over a little pot?* she wondered. All she knew was that the more she smoked, the more outrageously fabulous she felt.

Some of the marijuana smoked today can contain ten to 20 times more THC than there was in the pot smoked in the 1960s.

Inside the brain, each neuron (nerve cell) generates tiny electrical signals. Biochemicals called neurotransmitters shuttle between the neurons to pass along these signals until all the circuits needed to process and store a message— an image, sound, thought or sensation—have been completed.

Certain neurons, especially those that mediate balance, glucose craving and the perception of time, sound and color, have receptors that readily bind with THC. The THC molecules thus distort part of the brain's information-processing system, altering perception of time, while amplifying sounds and visual images.

As Heather's freshman year—and her use of marijuana—progressed, pot was no longer just a social drug. First thing in the morning, she smoked a joint to get herself out of bed. She smoked in a friend's car on the way to school. Between classes she smoked in the bathroom. She was even stoned when she sang in a school choir concert.

To achieve a high, meanwhile, required ever increasing amounts of the substance. She graduated to using a bong, or water pipe, which concentrates the smoke inside a chamber so none is lost into the air. "The only thing wasted," a bong purveyor promised, "is you."

Heather didn't worry that she needed more and more of the stuff. To her, this was a sign of prowess. "Look how much I can smoke and not get loaded," she bragged. And she downplayed thoughts of addiction. Pot, her friends kept reminding her, wasn't any more habit-forming than milk. She was sure she could quit any time.

The interaction of THC with brain receptors triggers intracellular signals that produce the high experienced by marijuana users. Among chronic users, continued bombardment of the cells by THC may lead to a tolerance for the drug. When this happens, the user needs more and more pot to get high.

Heather no longer cared about anyone or anything—except her next high.

When Heather's parents asked how school was going, she always flashed a big smile. "Everything's fine," she'd say. Because she'd always been such a good daughter, Frank and Diana Brooks had every reason to believe her. Gradually, though, Heather had become a highly accomplished liar.

"I'll be at Amy's house after school," she said one morning, looking her mother squarely in the eye. Instead, Heather drove with her friends to a dead-end dirt road where they smoked pot until it was time to go home for dinner.

On Friday nights, Heather came home promptly at her eleven o'clock curfew and said good-night to her parents. After the sliver of light under their door went out, she waited ten minutes, then tiptoed downstairs and slipped out the door to go party.

When Heather's gang smoked pot, they also always drank—beer or tumblers of vodka and cranberry juice. The alcohol made Heather feel more mellow than ever. It also amazed her how much she could drink without ever getting sick.

THC and alcohol together have a greater effect than either by itself. While marijuana distorts information processing, alcohol enhances the effects of a neurotransmitter called GABA, which binds to neurons and slows their rate of firing, producing a sedative effect.

THC also can reduce nausea. Vomiting is the body's natural way of purging toxic substances. If the vomit message is suppressed, as it is during marijuana use, dangerous amounts of alcohol can remain, in rare cases causing alcohol poisoning, organ damage and even death. While Heather considered it a "perk" that she could down so much beer while smoking pot, her body was like a guitar string about to snap.

At school Heather's absences began to mount and her grades took a nose dive. Yet for a while she continued to fool her parents. When report cards were mailed, she intercepted them at home and, with skillful use of correction fluid and a photocopying machine, turned D's and F's to A's and B's. She even added some nice comments: "Heather is a pleasure to have in class," she wrote, imitating the handwriting of one of her teachers.

By the end of Heather's freshman year, her grade-point average had plummeted from 4.0 to 1.2, and she'd tallied up a staggering 39 absences.

Meanwhile, Heather dropped many of her extracurricular activities. When her parents asked why, she said she just needed some "space." Diana and Frank Brooks pinned this on normal teen-age turmoil.

By now, Heather no longer cared about anyone or anything—except her next high. Her drive and motivation were gone, replaced by total apathy.

Drugs had become her life. She couldn't stop. In her journal she wrote: "Pot is a motionless sea of destruction. I'm drowning."

Indeed, always in excellent health, Heather now felt sick much of the time. Her hands and feet were constantly cold. She woke up coughing and pushed her face deep into her pillow so her parents wouldn't hear her. She also noticed that her menstrual cycle had become irregular.

Heather's parents saw the changes in their daughter. But their questions turned up nothing, and they were worried.

Marijuana Use Among Youths Ages 12–17

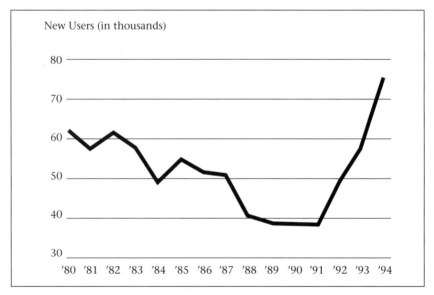

Source: Substance Abuse and Mental Health Services Administration Office of Applied Studies, U.S. Department of Health and Human Services.

Some studies show that deep inside the brain, THC may suppress the neurons of the hippocampus—where short-term memories are processed and sent to other brain areas for storage. As a result, the ability to learn and to remember recent events may be hampered.

Smoking marijuana can deliver three times more tar than smoking tobacco. Its irritating smoke dilates blood vessels; it also reddens the eyes and inflames delicate nasal tissues. Regular use can lead to chronic bronchitis.

Based on animal and in vitro studies using both human and animal mate-

rial, it's possible that pot may impair the capacity of the white cells to fight invading infection.

Moreover, the drug tinkers with the appetite center in the brain stem, which causes bouts of the "munchies"—a craving for sugary food.

Marijuana's final insult is to the pituitary gland, which regulates sex hormones. In men, some studies show sperm production can drop. And in women, ovulation may be inhibited.

Few people experiment with other illicit drugs without having tried marijuana first.

By her sophomore year, Heather knew all the tricks. To hide the smell of pot in her room, she stuffed an empty paper-towel roll with a sheet of fabric softener and exhaled into the tube. She carried eye drops to clear up bloodshot eyes. Before heading home, she gargled with mouthwash or chewed cinnamon-flavored gum. Often she brought a clean shirt to a party and left the smoke-saturated one behind.

As Heather's pot intake increased, she wanted even more. Encouraged by her friends, she experimented with a variety of mind-altering substances: LSD, mescaline, crack, codeine, cocaine and amphetamines. Through it all, however, marijuana remained her "drug of choice." It was what she started out with, and what she ended up with.

Studies show that there are developmental stages in drug use, though one drug doesn't inevitably lead to the next stage of abuse. A marijuana user most likely started with alcohol and cigarettes. Researchers say few people experiment with other illicit drugs without having tried marijuana first. A 1994 analysis showed that adults who used pot as children are 17 times more likely to become regular cocaine users.

One warm night toward the end of Heather's sophomore year, she attended what had become a typical party for her: the host's parents were away, and there was plenty of liquor along with a variety of drugs. Heather wasn't supposed to be there. Through conferences with her guidance counselor, her parents had found out about her doctored grades and her frequent absences. They now suspected alcohol or drugs and grounded her. But that evening her parents had gone out. Heather figured she could slip away and be back before they returned.

Around 10 p.m., she hopped in the back seat of a car with four others for a ride home. Ryan, the driver, was both drunk and stoned. As he stomped on the accelerator on a straight stretch of highway, Heather saw the speedometer pass 100 m.p.h.

Moments later, the car slammed into a guardrail, rolled down an embankment and came to rest on its roof. Miraculously, everyone survived. Ryan's face was jammed onto the steering-wheel horn, which blared loudly. Others bled from their faces and dangled broken limbs. Numbed by alcohol, marijuana and cocaine, Heather was oblivious of her own injuries as she helped one of her friends from the tangled wreck.

When a person is suddenly injured, neurotransmitters called endorphins lock on to natural opiate receptors in the brain and temporarily block out pain. Marijuana is an analgesic, which provides another method for muting pain.

Heather had suffered severe injuries to her back and neck, and would need a year of physical therapy.

"I didn't know Ryan had been drinking," Heather lied to her parents. They wanted desperately to believe her. Relieved that she was alive, they forgave her "just this once" for sneaking out. From then on, they warned, they were tightening their watch. But while she recuperated at home, Heather smoked pot secretly.

Heather had been dating Charlie Evans. He was handsome, athletic and popular with the girls. He was also heavily into marijuana and cocaine.

One evening three months after her accident, Charlie appeared at the front door with an eight-ball of cocaine (about an eighth of an ounce). Her parents were out to dinner. Soon Heather and Charlie were sniffing the white powder through straws.

After several lines, her heart began to race, something that had never happened before. She smoked a few joints to "mellow out," but instead she became more jumpy. Looking down, she saw her shirt move with the heavy pounding of her heart. Terrified, she told Charlie to call for help.

He dialed 911. "Send someone quick," he yelled. He didn't wait around. "I've got to split before the cops get here," he said, going out the back door.

En route to the hospital, Heather's heart rate soared to 196 beats a minute. "Talk to us," a paramedic urged. "We don't want to lose you."

Pot is a double-edged sword: it raises the heart's oxygen needs while lowering its supply. Just ten drags on a marijuana cigarette can overstimulate the heart muscle enough to push the heart rate from a normal 70 beats a minute to 100 beats and higher. The heart then needs more oxygen. Yet marijuana also elevates carbon monoxide levels in the blood, diminishing oxygen supply. Cocaine, meanwhile, causes the heart to beat inefficiently and its vessels to narrow. With Heather, the combination of drugs made her heart race dangerously out of control.

Finding Heather in intensive care and learning that she'd overdosed on cocaine, Diana Brooks broke into anguished cries. This was the wakeup call that Heather had long needed—and her parents too. "You've hit rock bottom," Frank told his daughter later. "We're still your best friends—but we're going to be watching you every minute."

Each morning, Frank Brooks waited to leave for work until Heather was on her bus. When she returned, a parent was waiting for her. No more rides with friends. No more parties.

That summer, her parents took her to a La Jolla, Calif., beach house to get her away from her "friends." For four full weeks, Heather was shaky, nervous and sweaty as her body adjusted to a healthier lifestyle. She had so much difficulty adapting to any kind of schedule that she wasn't sure when to eat or sleep. Slowly, however, her numbed brain began to function. Frequently, she thought about the time she spent in the hospital: *I almost died, and none of my friends even came to visit.*

Returning to Chicago, Heather was as determined to turn her life around as she once seemed determined to destroy it. She doubled up on courses she had failed as a sophomore. The sounds of her piano once again filled the Brooks home.

As a senior, Heather traveled to Europe with the school choir. As she stood in an ancient cathedral, her soprano voice joining the others, she recalled the concert when she'd shown up stoned.

Just three years ago, she thought. *What a different person I am now.*

Heather Brooks will always bear scars from her dance with the devil. She still has back pain from the accident, and occasionally she sees after-images trailing behind moving objects, a legacy of her drug use.

But her hopes are as big as they once were. In 1995 she entered college, where she maintains high grades. She hopes to attend law school.

"It was a close call," she says today. *"I almost let my dreams go up in a cloud of sweet-smelling smoke."*

Names and some details have been changed to protect privacy. For his assistance in preparing this article, Reader's Digest *thanks Prof. David H. Farb, Ph.D., chairman of the Department of Pharmacology, Boston University School of Medicine.*

3

Making Marijuana a Medical Issue Undercuts the Rationale of Legalization

Thomas S. Szasz

Thomas S. Szasz is professor emeritus of psychiatry at the State University of New York at Syracuse. A longtime critic of the psychiatric profession, he has written many books, including Ceremonial Chemistry, the Ritual Persecution of Drugs, Addicts, and Pushers *and* Our Right to Drugs: The Case for a Free Market.

Both opponents and supporters of marijuana prohibition fail to grasp the implications of the political movement to allow doctors to prescribe marijuana for medical use. The medical marijuana movement betrays the cause of drug legalization by placing control of drugs in the hands of physicians. Those who believe in a society where people are free to determine and take responsibility for their own drug use should oppose it.

D rug prohibitionists were alarmed last November 1996, when voters in Arizona and California endorsed the initiatives permitting the use of marijuana for "medical purposes." Opponents of drug prohibition ought to be even more alarmed: The advocates of medical marijuana have embraced a tactic that retards the repeal of drug prohibition and reinforces the moral legitimacy of prevailing drug policies. Instead of steadfastly maintaining that the War on Drugs is an intrinsically evil enterprise, the reformers propose replacing legal sanctions with medical tutelage, a principle destined to further expand the medical control of everyday behavior.

Not surprisingly, the drug prohibition establishment reacted to the passage of the marijuana initiatives as the Vatican might react to an outbreak of heretical schism. Senator Orrin G. Hatch, chairman of the Senate Judiciary Committee, declared: "We can't let this go without a response." Arizona Senator Jon Kyl told the Judiciary Committee: "I am extraordinarily embarrassed," adding that he believed most Arizona voters who supported the initiative "were deceived." Naturally. Only a per-

Reprinted from Thomas S. Szasz, "Medics in the War on Drugs," *Liberty*, March 1997, by permission of *Liberty*.

son who had fallen into error could approve of sin. Too many critics of the War on Drugs continue to refuse to recognize that their adversaries are priests waging a holy war on Satanic chemicals, not statesmen who respect the people and whose sole aim is to give them access to the best possible information concerning the benefits and risks of biologically active substances.

Taking drug decisions away from individuals

From Colonial times until 1914, Americans were the authors of their own drug policy: They decided what substances to avoid or use, controlled the drug-using behavior of their children, and assumed responsibility for their personal conduct. Since 1914, the control of, and assumed responsibility for, drug use—by adults as well as children—has been gradually transferred from citizens to agents of the state, principally physicians.

Supporters of the marijuana initiatives portray their policies as acts of compassion "to help the chronically or terminally ill." James E. Copple, president of Community Anti-Drug Coalitions of America, counters: "They are using the AIDS victims and terminally ill as props to promote the use of marijuana." He is right. Former Surgeon General Joycelyn Elders declares: "I think that we can really legalize marijuana." If by "legalizing" she means repealing marijuana prohibition, then she does not know what she is talking about. We have sunk so low in the War on Drugs that, at present, legalizing marijuana in the United States is about as practical as is legalizing Scotch in Saudi Arabia. A 1995 Gallup Poll found that 85 percent of the respondents opposed legalizing illicit drugs.

Instead of steadfastly maintaining that the War on Drugs is an intrinsically evil enterprise, the reformers propose replacing legal sanctions with medical tutelage.

Supporters of the marijuana initiatives are posturing as advocates of medical "responsibility" toward "sick patients." Physicians complain of being deprived of their right to free speech. It won't work. The government can out-responsible the doctors any day. Physicians have "prescription privileges," a euphemism for what is, in effect, the power to issue patients *ad hoc* licenses to buy certain drugs. This makes doctors major players in the state apparatus denying people their rights to drugs, thereby denying them the option of responsible drug use and abdicating their own responsibilities to the government: "We will not turn a blind eye toward our responsibility," declared Attorney General Janet Reno at a news conference on December 30, 1996, where the administration announced "that doctors in California and Arizona who ordered for their patients any drugs like marijuana . . . could lose their prescription privileges and even face criminal charges." I don't blame the doctors for wanting to forget the Satanic pact they have forged with the state, but they should not expect the government not to remind them of it.

The American people as well as their elected representatives support the War on Drugs. The mainstream media addresses the subject in a language that precludes rational debate: crimes related to drug prohibition are systematically described as "drug-related." Perhaps most important, Americans in ever-increasing numbers seem to be deeply, almost religiously, committed to a medicalized view of life. Thus, Dennis Peron, the originator of the California marijuana proposition, believes that since relieving stress is beneficial to health, "any adult who uses marijuana does so for medical reasons." Similarly, Ethan Nadelmann, director of the Lindesmith Center (the George Soros think tank for drug policy), states: "The next step is toward arguing for a more rational drug policy," such as distributing hypodermic needles and increasing access to methadone for heroin addicts. These self-declared opponents of the War on Drugs are blind to the fatal compromise entailed in their use of the phrase "rational policy."

If we believe we have a right to a free press, we do not seek a rational book policy or reading policy; on the contrary, we would call such a policy "censorship" and a denial of our First Amendment rights.

If we believe we have a right to freedom of religion, we do not seek a rational belief policy or religion policy; on the contrary, we would call such a policy "religious persecution" and a denial of the constitutionally mandated separation of church and state.

So long as we do not believe in freedom of, and responsibility for, drug use, we cannot mount an effective opposition to medical-statist drug controls. In a free society, the duty of the government is to protect individuals from others who might harm them; it is not the government's business to protect individuals from harming themselves. Misranking these governmental functions precludes the possibility of repealing our drug laws. Presciently, C.S. Lewis warned against yielding to the temptations of medical tutelage: "Of all the tyrannies a tyranny sincerely exercised for the good of its victims may be the most oppressive. . . . To be 'cured' against one's will and cured of states which we may not regard as disease is to be put on a level with those who have not yet reached the age of reason or those who never will; to be classed with infants, imbeciles, and domestic animals."

Although at present we cannot serve the cause of liberty by repealing the drug laws, we can betray that cause by supporting the fiction that self-medication is a disease, prohibiting it is a public health measure, and punishing it is a treatment.

4

Full Legalization Is the Agenda of the Medical Marijuana Movement

Michael J. Meyers

Michael J. Meyers is a drug-addiction physician at Kaiser Permanente in Carson, California.

While further research on the possible medical benefits of marijuana should be considered, people should realize that marijuana is a potentially dangerous and addictive mood-altering substance. Proponents of marijuana are exploiting the suffering of patients to support their own agenda of legalizing all marijuana use, resulting in public confusion and in poorly written laws such as California's Proposition 215 initiative.

"Marijuana is a mood-altering drug capable of producing dependence. This basic assertion . . . has not been altered by recent passage of California's Proposition 215 . . . [which is] poorly written and unimplementable without further enabling and clarifying legislation. Implementing legislation and regulatory changes creating appropriate safeguards [both for physicians and patients] is required on both the state and federal levels. . . . The California Society of Addiction Medicine [CSAM] urges all California physicians to adhere voluntarily to these standards."
—from *CSAM News* (Spring 1997)

"Marijuana has been shown to have adverse effects on various organ systems, on perception, behavior, functioning, and on fetal development. Because of the widespread use of this drug, its effects on mind and body, and the increasing potency of available supplies, [the American Society of Addiction Medicine] strongly recommends that approved medical use of marijuana or delta-9-tetrahydrocannabinol for treatment of illnesses . . . or other uses should be carefully controlled. The drug should be administered only under the supervision of a knowledgeable physician. Research on marijuana, including both basic science and applied clinical

Reprinted from Michael J. Meyers, "A Reasoned Argument," *Professional Counselor*, October 1997, by permission of the author.

studies, should receive increased funding and appropriate access to marijuana for the study. The mechanisms of action of marijuana, its effect on the human body, its addictive properties, and any appropriate medical applications should be investigated, and the results made known for clinical and policy applications. In addition, ASAM strongly encourages research related to the potential and actual effects of marijuana-related public policy. ASAM encourages the study of the potential impact of making cannabis available for approved medical uses, and the consideration of what changes might result from moving cannabis from Schedule I to another schedule."

—from a position statement by the
American Society of Addiction Medicine

As one of the lead authors of the rebuttal argument against Proposition 215, which appeared in voter-information packets in California prior to the November 1996 election, I continue to be approached by the media as a likely candidate to combat the organizers and proponents of this proposition, who convinced a majority of the electorate to pass the so-called "medical marijuana" initiative.

They are soon disappointed, however, when I go on to explain that I was specifically against this particular proposition on the grounds that it is poorly written legislation. In fact, I am totally for additional funding and research to determine the efficacy and safety of cannabis as a therapeutic agent. This information usually propels them to seek out someone else more suitable to counter the hyperbole and pseudoscience of the proponents on the other side of the issue.

The pro-legalization folks need to . . . stop using the suffering and death of patients . . . as a wedge to drive home their own agenda.

As someone who has been vilified and charged with everything from being "a pimp for the greedy pharmaceutical companies" to a "hired gun for the government drug warriors" to the cruelest cut of all, a Republican (me, a card-carrying American Civil Liberties Union [ACLU] member and leftover '60s hippie), I welcome the opportunity to present the position of the two organizations that represent my specialty, addiction medicine. I especially appreciate the thoughtful balance between acknowledging that marijuana is a psychoactive, mood- and mind-altering substance that can certainly serve as a gateway to the use of more destructive psychoactive substances, and yet recognizing that these factors should not preclude its potential use as a therapeutic agent. It remains the responsibility of professional addiction medicine societies to keep the issue in perspective by documenting the addictive qualities of marijuana, and by safeguarding its use for those for whom it may be justified by challenging the exaggerated claims of its harmfulness.

The proponents of Proposition 215 are using bait-and-switch tactics to brazenly (though not too publicly) advance their true agenda: using the "medical marijuana" issue as a stepping stone toward legalization of all marijuana use. There is certainly need for public debate regarding drug policies, harm reduction, decriminalization, and the like. However, a Chinese proverb states that 90 percent of all knowledge is calling things by their right name.

The pro-legalization folks need to come out from behind the straw horse and stop using the suffering and death of patients who can truly benefit from marijuana as a wedge to drive home their own agenda.

5

The Government
War on Marijuana
Should Be Maintained

Mark Souder

Mark Souder is a Republican member of Congress representing Indiana. As vice-chairman of the House Government Reform and Oversight Subcommittee on National Security, he has been active in overseeing U.S. government efforts against illegal drug trafficking.

Proponents of marijuana legalization are attempting to con voters with deceptive referenda on medical marijuana. But marijuana should not be smoked as medicine because it is a harmful and addictive substance that can cause respiratory disease, mental disorders, and other health problems. Marijuana can also lead to abuse of other drugs. The government should keep marijuana illegal and strengthen its efforts to prohibit it.

*R*olling Stone magazine noted in its May 5, 1994, issue that currency speculator and billionaire philanthropist George Soros gave the Drug Policy Foundation, one of many recipients of his "charitable" largesse, suggestions to follow if they wanted his assistance: "[H]ire someone with the political savvy to sit down and negotiate with government officials and target a few winnable issues, like medical marijuana and the repeal of mandatory minimums." Keith Stroup, founder of the National Organization for the Reform of Marijuana Laws, or NORML, told an Emory University audience in 1979 that medicinal marijuana would be used as a red herring to give marijuana a good name. Richard Cowan, writing for the pro-drug *High Times* magazine, described the "medical model as spearheading a strategy for the legalization of marijuana by 1997."

According to public-opinion polls, legalization of marijuana is not supported by the American people. This explains why the drug lobby carefully steers away from using the term "legalization," preferring cryptic terms such as harm reduction, decriminalization and medicalization.

The goal of the drug lobby has not changed; it only is camouflaged. The public sensibly and resolutely remains opposed to recreational marijuana use, but drug legalizers shamefully are trying to con voters through deceptive ballot referenda exploiting the ill and dying.

Marijuana legalizers commonly claim America's prisons teem with young people whose only crime was simple possession of marijuana, and that drug arrests disproportionately affect minorities. The debate about crack-cocaine sentencing disparities sparked similar claims of racism by the criminal-justice system. The drug lobby ignores the obvious fact that a war on drugs hits inner-city traffickers foremost and helps law-abiding residents of neighborhoods who have the least resources with which to fight back. Despite the inescapable conclusion that placing drug dealers behind bars protects neighborhoods against criminals, violent crime and social ills attendant with drug use, drug legalizers such as University of California at Los Angeles' Mark Kleiman absurdly claim: "Locking up a burglar does not materially change the opportunities for other burglars, while locking up a drug dealer leaves potential customers for new dealers."

Legalization of marijuana is not supported by the American people.

The drug lobby frequently compares the drug war to Prohibition. But as a publication at the turn of the century (when the United States had a raging drug problem) observed, "a drunkard may retain his moral equilibrium between debauches . . . but the 'dope fiend,' once thoroughly addicted, inevitably drops into utter debasement." Unlike illegal drugs, alcohol and drinking were embedded in Anglo-Saxon and European social customs. While the temperance movement prevailed after heated debate, drug restrictions passed during the same period widely were regarded as uncontroversial and needed. Western states passed marijuana-prohibition laws in response to a rash of crimes and violence linked to cannabis use among Mexican immigrants. A medical exemption existed then to the import of marijuana, but soon states and politicians appealed to the federal government for help in confronting the "loco weed." Legendary New York journalist Meyer Berger in 1938 summed up expert medical opinion at the time: "Marijuana, while no more habit-forming than ordinary cigarette smoking, offers a shorter cut to complete madness than any other drug."

Drug legalizers recently lost a ballot initiative in Washington state on Nov. 4, [1997] a setback from victories to legalize illegal drugs last year in California and Arizona. The Washington-state referendum—I-685, which failed by a margin of 60 percent to 40 percent—combined the worst aspects of the legalization initiatives in California and Arizona by not only seeking to legalize marijuana but also cocaine, heroin, LSD and other narcotics on Schedule I of the federal Controlled Substances Act, drugs judged to have no medicinal benefit and high potential for abuse. I-685 also would have released drug offenders from prison. I-685 was bolstered by millions of dollars in contributions from a handful of out-of-state millionaires, including Soros—dubbed the "Daddy Warbucks" of drug legalization by former health, education and welfare secretary Joe Califano—

and Arizona millionaire John Sperling. The measure failed even though drug legalizers outspent antidrug advocates by a ratio of nearly 15-to-1.

Washington state antidrug activists warned against complacency in fighting the legalizers. They acknowledged the battle against I-685 was significantly buoyed by the zealotry of the legalizers to delist Schedule I substances and by the National Rifle Association's successful multimillion-dollar campaign against a gun-control referendum also on the ballot.

The problem with ballot initiatives

The District of Columbia is threatened with a marijuana "medicalization" initiative in November 1998, sponsored by a homosexual advocacy organization, the AIDS Coalition to Unleash Power. AIDS activists should take note of pioneering research by Dr. Thomas Klein at the University of South Florida who showed marijuana alters the immune system and may accelerate HIV-infection into full-blown AIDS cases. D.C.'s Measure 57 would permit up to 20 people to cultivate and sell unlimited quantities of marijuana for an individual suffering from an amorphous range of conditions—essentially shielding drug dealers from prosecution.

As drug czar Barry McCaffrey argues, the ballot box is the wrong place for decisions about efficacy and safety of medicines. The Food and Drug Administration, or FDA, was created to protect the public against snake-oil salesmen, and consumer-safety laws require proper labeling of ingredients and dosages. The sale of crude marijuana circumvents those protections.

The pro-drug lobby successfully described Proposition 215 in California as "medical" marijuana for the sick and dying, preying on the compassionate nature of the American people, but Prop. 215 legalized marijuana with no age limitation for "any illness for which marijuana provides relief," including ailments of dubious nature and severity such as memory recall, writers cramp and corn calluses. The FDA has approved the only psychoactive ingredient of marijuana, THC, found useful for pain relief as Marinol, in pill form through prescription. Marinol, a Schedule II drug with limited medical use and high potential for abuse, is an antinausea drug for cancer patients who fail to respond to other drugs, and an appetite stimulant for people suffering from AIDS wasting syndrome. THC has not, however, been shown to be safe and effective for any other condition other than nausea and wasting due to AIDS. In a double-blind study, patients preferred Marinol over smoking marijuana 2-to-1. A marijuana study by the Institute of Medicine concluded risks of marijuana on the immune system were such that it favored development of a smoke-free inhaled delivery system to provide purer forms of THC, or its related compound, cannabinoids.

Why people should not consider marijuana to be medicine

The drug lobby, however, rejects legal use of THC in Marinol and continues to promote use of crude marijuana cigarettes as medicine. One doctor, explaining why marijuana is not medicine, gave the analog of eating moldy bread in an attempt to get penicillin. A prominent oncologist professed he could manage pain with legal drugs in 99 percent of his patients, and that there are newer and better medications for chemotherapy patients than Marinol, describing one, Zofran, as a "miracle" drug.

Crude marijuana consists of more than 400 chemicals which, when smoked, become thousands of chemicals. Drugs from a pharmacy are of a single ingredient and of a known dosage. Pot advocates often cite the fact that morphine, available under a doctor's care, is a heroin derivative. What they neglect to mention is that morphine received FDA approval and underwent rigorous clinical testing, a public-safety standard approved drugs must meet.

Drug legalizers often cite Americans participating in an ongoing federal experiment at the University of Mississippi to evaluate any benefit from medicinal marijuana, implying that the federal government believes marijuana could be medicinal. But to date, despite 12,000 studies of the medical utility of marijuana, an overwhelming consensus exists in the scientific community that smoked marijuana never can be a medicine. The federal experimental program, consisting of eight people, has declined new admissions since 1992. Congress, in its reauthorization of the drug-czar's office, banned further studies of marijuana as medicine, a provision which I sponsored.

Marijuana is addictive, leading to the use of other drugs such as cocaine an... heroin.

While the Clinton administration campaigns vigorously against cigarettes and chides the tobacco industry for its marketing techniques, marijuana cigarettes rarely are targets of condemnation. Ironically, the tobacco industry, like the drug lobby today, once promoted cigarettes as medicine until the Federal Trade Commission halted this practice in 1955.

Marijuana is addictive, leading to the use of other drugs such as cocaine and heroin, and is a major cause of accidents and injuries. It can cause respiratory disease and mental disorders including depression, paranoia, decreased cognitive performance and impaired memory. Babies born to women who smoked marijuana during pregnancy have an increased incidence of leukemia, low birth weight and other newborn abnormalities. The National Institute of Drug Abuse's director frequently mentions brain scans showing that lower cerebral activity seems to account for some of the reported learning disturbances found in chronic marijuana users.

As a *New York Times* editorial put it, parents need to realize today's marijuana is more potent than the version they may have smoked in their youth, and "research has shown the drug to be far more dangerous to young people than was known in the 1960s and 1970s, with a higher THC content. It can be particularly harmful to the growth and development of teenagers."

There is a solid reason for scientific studies and FDA approval—to avoid medical catastrophes such as thalidomide. Good medicine is not conceived at the polls, but through routine clinical trials. Since marijuana is far more carcinogenic than tobacco cigarettes, it's not compassionate to recommend it to sick people—it's cruel.

6

Marijuana Is Safe and Effective Medicine

Lester Grinspoon and James B. Bakalar

Lester Grinspoon is a professor of psychiatry at Harvard Medical School. James B. Bakalar is a lecturer in law at the department of psychiatry at Harvard Medical School. They are coauthors of the book Marihuana, the Forbidden Medicine.

Cannabis is a safe and versatile medicine that has many possible medical uses. Anecdotal evidence—the source of much medical knowledge—suggests that it can relieve vomiting in cancer chemotherapy, restore appetite in AIDS patients, and help people suffering from glaucoma, epilepsy, Crohn's disease, mood disorders, and other diseases. Marijuana is less toxic or dangerous than most prescription medicines. Physicians have the obligation to provide informative answers to patients' questions about marijuana and to challenge government policies preventing its use.

In November 1996 the people of California approved Proposition 215, an initiative that could, in effect, make marihuana legally available as a medicine in the United States for the first time in many years. Under the new law, patients or their primary caregivers who possess or cultivate marihuana for medical treatment recommended by a physician are exempted from criminal prosecution. The treatment may be for "cancer, anorexia, AIDS, chronic pain, spasticity, glaucoma, arthritis, migraine, or any other illness for which marihuana provides relief." Physicians may not be penalized in any way for making the recommendation, which may be either written or oral.[1] The passage of this law is only the beginning of a trend that presents new challenges for physicians, who will be asked to assume responsibilities for which many have not prepared themselves. As more and more patients approach them with questions about marihuana, they will have to provide answers and make recommendations. That means they must not only listen more carefully to their patients but educate themselves and one another. They will have to learn which symptoms

Reprinted from Lester Grinspoon and James B. Bakalar, "Marihuana: An Old Medicine of the Future," at www.rxmarihuana.com/old_medicine.htm, ©1997, by permission of the authors.

and disorders may be treated better with marihuana than with conventional medications, and they may need to explain how to use marihuana.

A safe and versatile medicine

Cannabis is a strikingly safe, versatile, and potentially inexpensive medicine. When we reviewed its medical uses in 1993 after examining many patients and case histories, we were able to list the following: nausea and vomiting in cancer chemotherapy, the weight loss syndrome of AIDS, glaucoma, epilepsy, muscle spasms and chronic pain in multiple sclerosis, quadriplegia and other spastic disorders, migraine, severe pruritus, depression, and other mood disorders.[2] Since then we have identified more than a dozen others, including asthma, insomnia, dystonia, scleroderma, Crohn's disease, diabetic gastroparesis, and terminal illness. The list is not exhaustive.[3]

For example, cannabis has also been found useful in the treatment of osteoarthritis. Aspirin is believed to cause more than 1,000 deaths annually in the United States. More than 7,600 annual deaths and 70,000 hospitalizations caused by non-steroidal anti-inflammatory drugs (NSAIDs) are reported. Gastrointestinal complications of NSAIDs are the most commonly reported serious adverse drug reaction.[4] Long-term acetaminophen use is thought to be one of the most common causes of end-stage renal disease.[5] Cannabis smoked several times a day is often as effective as NSAIDs or acetaminophen in osteoarthritis, and there have been no reports of death from cannabis.

Anecdotal evidence

It is often objected that the evidence of marihuana's medical usefulness, although powerful, is merely anecdotal. It is true that there are no studies meeting the standards of the Food and Drug Administration, chiefly because legal, bureaucratic, and financial obstacles are constantly put in the way. The situation is ironical, since so much research has been done on marihuana, often in unsuccessful efforts to show health hazards and addictive potential, that we know more about it than about most prescription drugs. In any case, controlled studies can be misleading if the wrong patients are studied or the wrong doses are used, and idiosyncratic therapeutic responses can be obscured in group experiments.

Cannabis is a strikingly safe, versatile, and potentially inexpensive medicine.

Anecdotal evidence is the source of much of our knowledge of drugs. As Louis Lasagna has pointed out, controlled experiments were not needed to recognize the therapeutic potential of chloral hydrate, barbiturates, aspirin, insulin, or penicillin.[6] Anecdotal evidence also revealed the usefulness of propranolol and chlorothiazide for hypertension, diazepam for status epilepticus, and imipramine for enuresis. All these drugs had originally been approved for other purposes.

Some physicians may regard it as irresponsible to support, let alone advocate the medical use of cannabis on the basis of anecdotal evidence, which seems to count successes and ignore failures. That would be a serious problem only if cannabis were a dangerous drug. The years of effort devoted to showing that marihuana is exceedingly dangerous have proved the opposite. It is safer, with fewer serious side effects, than most prescription medicines, and far less addictive or subject to abuse than many drugs now used as muscle relaxants, hypnotics, and analgesics.

The years of effort devoted to showing that marihuana is exceedingly dangerous have proved the opposite.

Thus it can be argued that even if only a few patients could get relief from cannabis, it should be made available because the risks would be so small. For example, many patients with multiple sclerosis find that cannabis reduces their muscle spasms and pain. A physician may not be sure that such a patient will get better relief from marihuana than from the baclofen, dantrolene, and high doses of diazepam that the patient has been taking, but it is certain that a serious toxic reaction to marihuana is extremely unlikely, and risk-benefit considerations therefore make it worth trying. However, some preparation and instruction may be required, both to realize therapeutic goals and to avoid unwanted reactions. The psychoactive effects, for example, must be explained to marihuana-naive patients, who may otherwise suffer some anxiety at first.

Comparing smoked and oral medicines

The chief legitimate concern is the effect of smoking on the lungs. Many physicians find it difficult to endorse a smoked medicine. Although cannabis smoke carries even more tars and other particulate matter than tobacco smoke, the amount needed by most patients is extremely limited. Furthermore, when marihuana is an openly recognized medicine, solutions for this problem may be found, perhaps by the development of a technique for inhaling cannabinoid vapors. Even today, the greatest danger of using marihuana medically is not impurities in the smoke but illegality, which imposes much unnecessary anxiety and expense on suffering people.

A synthetic version of delta-9-tetrahydrocannabinol, the main active substance in cannabis, has been available in oral form for limited purposes as a Schedule II drug since 1985. This medicine, dronabinol (Marinol), is generally regarded by both patients and physicians as less effective than smoked marihuana. A patient who is severely nauseated and constantly vomiting, for example, may find it almost impossible to keep a pill or capsule down. Oral THC is erratically and slowly absorbed into the bloodstream; the dose and duration of action of smoked marihuana are easier to titrate. Furthermore, oral THC occasionally makes many patients anxious and uncomfortable, possibly because cannabidiol, one of the many substances in marihuana, has an anxiolytic effect.[7]

Besides their direct responsibility to individual patients with respect to medical marihuana, physicians have another obligation that is social and ultimately political. Jerome P. Kassirer has identified it in his recent New England Journal of Medicine editorial entitled "Federal Foolishness and marihuana." He describes the government's policies on medical marihuana as "hypocritical" and predicts that physicians who "have the courage to challenge the continued proscription of marihuana for the sick" will eventually force the government to reach some sort of accommodation.[8] That important task will inevitably fall to the younger generation of doctors, including present and future medical students.

References

1. California Health and Safety Code Section 11362.5

2. Grinspoon L, Bakalar JB. *Marihuana, the Forbidden Medicine.* New Haven: Yale University Press, 1993.

3. Grinspoon L, Bakalar JB. *Marihuana, the Forbidden Medicine* (revised and enlarged edition). New Haven: Yale University Press, in press, 1997.

4. Gurkirpal S, Ramey DR, Morfeld D, Shi H, Hatoum HT, and Fries, JF. Gastrointestinal tract complications of nonsteroidal anti-inflammatory drug treatment in rheumatoid arthritis. *Archives of Internal Medicine* 1996; 156:1530–6.

5. Perneger TV, Whelton P, and Klag MJ. Risk of kidney failure associated with the use of acetaminophen, aspirin, and nonsteroidal anti-inflammatory drugs. *N Engl J Med* 1994;331:1675–9. Ronco PM, Falhault A. Drug-induced end-stage renal disease. Editorial, *N Engl J Med* 1994;331:1711–2.

6. Lasagna L. Clinical trials in the natural environment. In *Drugs between Research and Regulations,* ed. Stiechele C, Abshagen W, and Koch-Weser J. 1985. Darmstadt: Steinkopff Verlag, pp. 45–9.

7. Chang AE, et al. Delta-9-tetrahydrocannabinol as an antiemetic in cancer patients receiving high-dose methotrexate: a prospective, randomized evaluation. *Annals of Internal Medicine* 1979;91:819–24. Zuardi AW, Shirakawa I, Finkelbarb E, and Karnio IG. Action of cannabidiol on the anxiety and other effects produced by delta-9-THC in normal subjects. *Psychopharmacology* 1976;76:245–50.

8. Kassirer JP. Federal foolishness and marihuana. *N Engl J Med* 1997; 336:366–7.

7

Patients Suffering from Cancer and Other Ailments Should Be Allowed Marijuana

Richard Brookhiser

Richard Brookhiser is a senior editor of National Review, *a conservative magazine.*

The author ingested marijuana to obtain relief from nausea caused by chemotherapy treatments. Based on his experience, Brookhiser contends that marijuana should be made legally available to cancer victims like himself and other patients who could benefit from it. Arguments raised against medical marijuana are flawed; the pill form of marijuana's active ingredient is an inadequate substitute for smoked marijuana, and legalizing medical marijuana does not glamorize or encourage casual drug use. Regardless of the general merits of the government's war on drugs, sick people should not be forced to become lawbreakers in order to relieve their suffering.

I am a conservative Republican. I am a senior editor of *National Review*, Ronald Reagan's favorite magazine. I've written for it for 26 years. I support the use of medical marijuana because of my politics, but I'm also for it because I've had to use it.

In 1992 I got testicular cancer. The treatment was straightforward—an operation, followed by a rather harsh form of chemotherapy. Any chemotherapy is harsh because all chemotherapy is poison. You're dumping poison into your bloodstream, killing millions of cells, in order to kill the thousands of malignant cells which will not recover. Because it is poison, the body wants to get rid of it. That's why chemotherapy causes nausea. To deal with this, I took the latest anti-nausea drugs and I also did self-hypnosis and mental imaging. These all worked—up to a point. But beyond that point, I needed extra help and so I smoked marijuana.

Reprinted from Richard Brookhiser's congressional testimony before the Subcommittee on Crime, Committee on the Judiciary, U.S. House of Representatives, March 6, 1996.

I had smoked marijuana maybe ten times in college during the seventies. I even inhaled. I stopped because I found that I didn't like smoke, or being high, or the conversation of pot-heads. I turned to it again when I got cancer because marijuana gives healthy people an appetite and prevents people who are nauseated from throwing up. None of my doctors or nurses at New York University Medical Center or Memorial Sloan-Kettering discouraged me from doing this. They had all had patients who had used marijuana to fight nausea and who had reported good results. I had good results too. Because of the marijuana, my last two courses of chemotherapy were almost nausea-free.

There was only one problem; I had to become a criminal to do this. Cancer patients are not the only people in this bind. AIDS patients who have the wasting syndrome report that marijuana gives them an appetite again. Glaucoma patients find that it arrests the deterioration of their eyes. People with chronic migraines, epilepsy, and multiple sclerosis use it to relieve their symptoms. A good summary of all of these experiences can be found in *Marihuana, The Forbidden Medicine*, by Lester Grinspoon, M.D. and James B. Bakalar. Dr. Grinspoon is a professor of psychiatry at Harvard Medical School and the book is published by Yale University Press, so this is not something downloaded from the Internet. But any sick person who wants to use marijuana to help himself has to break the law. I'm a member of the media elite who lives in Manhattan so I wasn't at high risk. But plenty of sick people get arrested and plenty of them go to jail.

Three arguments against medical marijuana

There are three common arguments against the medical use of marijuana, all of them faulty.

1. The first is that THC, the main active ingredient in the drug, is available in a legally prescribable pill form. But the pill has problems. It's expensive. Because it's a pill, and therefore slower acting, people have trouble adjusting the dosage; they often find themselves taking too much. In my case, I thought treating nausea with a pill was not a bright idea.

2. The second argument is that smoked marijuana has never been tested scientifically. This is not entirely true. One test was done at UCLA in 1970 for the Los Angeles Police Department to prove that pot-smoking dilated the pupils. However, the researchers found that it actually contracted the pupils. They also discovered that marijuana relieved pressure within the eyeball. This is why marijuana is useful in treating glaucoma.

Any sick person who wants to use marijuana to help himself has to break the law.

But it is true that it is difficult to test marijuana. That is because the government makes it so. The case of Dr. Donald Abrams at San Francisco General Hospital is instructive. Dr. Abrams is an AIDS researcher who wants to test the efficacy of smoked marijuana in treating the wasting syndrome. For more than two years, he tried to get marijuana legally from the National Institute on Drug Abuse for his experiments—to no avail. So doctors cannot prescribe marijuana because it hasn't been tested, but doctors aren't allowed to do any tests. This is a classic "Catch-22."

3. The third objection is that by legalizing marijuana, we will be setting a bad example to a society engaged in a war on drugs. In fact, we will be setting no example at all. The availability of morphine in hospitals is not the reason people smoke crack. A hairless cancer patient with an IV tube in his arm is not a come-on for a pusher. The connection between the issue of medical marijuana and the war on drugs runs the other way. The reason we don't allow medical use is because of the spill-over of an extreme war-time psychology.

Republican principles and the war on drugs

National Review has taken a stand on the war on drugs, but it is not relevant here. If you think the war is wrong, then the ban on medical marijuana is simply one symptom among many of its excess and folly. If you think the war is right, then the ban is an irrelevant and over-zealous offshoot, like fighting the Kaiser in World War I by changing the German names of Midwestern streets.

I want to end by addressing my fellow Republicans. My support for medical marijuana is not a contradiction of my principles, but an extension of them. I am for law and order. But crime has to be fought intelligently and the law disgraces itself when it harasses the sick. I am for traditional virtues, but carrying your beliefs to unjust ends is not moral, it is philistine. Most importantly, I believe in getting government off people's backs. We should include the backs of sick people trying to help themselves.

My cancer is gone now, I was lucky. God forbid that anyone in this room should ever need chemotherapy, but statistics tell us that many of us will. Let me assure you that whatever you think now, or however you vote, if that moment comes to you, you will turn to marijuana. Extend that liberty to your fellow citizens.

8

The Government Should Be Cautious in Permitting the Medical Use of Marijuana

Barry McCaffrey

Barry McCaffrey, a retired U.S. Army general, was appointed by President Bill Clinton to be director of the Office of National Drug Control Policy—the nation's "drug czar"—in 1996.

Federal government policy toward marijuana must be based on science, not ideology. Scientific tests and the appropriate government agencies—not public votes such as those in California and Arizona—should determine whether marijuana is safe and effective medicine. Public endorsements of medical marijuana send the wrong message to America's youth about its potential for harm. The government should keep marijuana a controlled substance because of the dangers it poses, especially to young people.

Editor's note: The following viewpoint is taken from Barry McCaffrey's statement on the federal government's response to medical marijuana referenda, submitted for the record to the House Judiciary Committee, Subcommittee on Crime, on October 1, 1997.

Chairman Bill McCollum, members of the subcommittee, thank you for the opportunity to address the issue of medical marijuana referenda in the United States. The Office of National Drug Control Policy (ONDCP) is pleased to work with the 105th Congress to dramatically reduce drug use and its consequences. In particular, Chairman McCollum, the Office of National Drug Control Policy appreciates your longstanding support, as well as that of this committee's members. Indeed, the Office of National Drug Control Policy Reauthorization Act of 1997, which is now before the Congress reflects a continuing and constructive dialogue between committed Senators and Representatives, their expert staff, and ONDCP. Over the past 17 years since 1980, bipartisan partnership has

Reprinted from Barry McCaffrey's statement submitted to the Subcommittee on Crime, Committee on the Judiciary, U.S. House of Representatives, October 1, 1997.

contributed to a 50 percent overall reduction in drug use and a 75 percent reduction in casual cocaine use. Nevertheless, America's drug abuse problem will kill another 140,000 Americans and cost our society $700 billion over the coming decade if unchecked. My commitment to the Congress when you considered my appointment in February of 1996 remains constant—to forge a coherent counter drug strategy that will reduce illegal drug use and protect our youth and society in general from the terrible damage caused by drug abuse and drug trafficking.

The federal response to marijuana referenda

Today, it is my purpose to update you on developments since early December 1996, when we addressed the issue of medical marijuana referenda before the Senate Committee on the Judiciary. The ballot initiatives passed in November of 1996 in Arizona and California bypassed the rigorous scientific approval process required of all medicines and allowed for the use of marijuana as a "medicine." President Bill Clinton directed ONDCP to lead an interagency task force responsible for developing a sound federal response. Members of this task force included: ONDCP and the departments of Justice, Treasury, Defense, Health and Human Services, Transportation, Labor, Education, and the Postal Service, and the Nuclear Regulatory Commission. ONDCP also sought input from prominent medical experts, elected state and local officials, Congressional delegations, drug prevention and treatment groups, law enforcement officials, community leaders, and concerned citizens. On December 30, 1996, the federal response was announced at a press conference with Attorney General Janet Reno, Health and Human Services Secretary Donna Shalala, Director of the National Institute on Drug Abuse, Dr. Alan Leshner, and myself.

I. A Federal Response Based on Science, Not Ideology

The logic of the federal response is simple: federal law remains in effect, and science must prevail over ideology. At the heart of the federal response is the preservation of the longstanding, established medical-scientific process for ensuring that any substance purporting to be a medicine must undergo the rigorous evaluation of the scientific process. This process has protected American citizens from snake oils, dangerous drugs, unproven substances and ineffective treatments for over fifty years. Because of this process, American citizens have faith that the drugs they take are both safe and effective. The government's position is that any substance provided or sold to the American public as a medicine must withstand the scrutiny of the same medical-scientific process to which all other potential medicines are subject. To exempt any substance from this time-honored procedure will undermine the established process that has long protected the American public so well.

The federal response on medical marijuana has four goals: 1) preserving the established scientific medical process for determining safe and effective medicines; 2) protecting our youth; 3) upholding existing federal law; and, 4) preserving drug-free workplaces. . . .

A. What Constitutes Good Medicine Should Not be Determined at the Ballot Box

Referenda cannot protect American citizens from fraudulent claims and dangerous drugs. Nor can they ensure that potential medicines are subjected to a process of evaluation by both the Food and Drug Administration (FDA) and the National Institute of Health (NIH) based on sound science. A fundamental role of the FDA is to protect the public's health and safety by testing every potential medicine to ensure both their safety and efficacy. For a purely medical and scientific issue to be decided by popular referendum undercuts the safeguards established over the years by the Congress through the federal Pure Food and Drug Laws. Subverting the public health process and declaring smoked marijuana a "medicine" threatens the integrity of our established medical safeguards.

This issue has nothing to do with marijuana specifically; rather, it has everything to do with protecting the public health and safety of our citizens. Avram Goldstein, M.D., Professor Emeritus of Pharmacology at Stanford University, offers the following analogy: Imagine a ballot initiative to change the rules by which the Federal Aeronautics and Aviation (FAA)'s Air Traffic Control System manages commercial aircraft in California. It is disturbing to think that well-funded activists in one state could establish different procedures from the rest of the country on a matter that clearly affects the well-being of all of us. If *sound* medical research demonstrates that there are medical uses for smoked marijuana, there are appropriate and responsive procedures for rescheduling this mind-influencing drug through the time-tested process. The FDA has already demonstrated flexibility in accelerating procedures for allowing the use of emerging AIDS-related drugs without jeopardizing science or the public health.

Declaring smoked marijuana a "medicine" threatens the integrity of our established medical safeguards.

B. Protecting the American Public from Unproven Substances is Our Shared Responsibility

The medical process for establishing substances as medications is well established and clear: the FDA evaluates clinical and laboratory data developed and submitted by outside scientists and clinicians to determine if the scientific evidence demonstrates that the benefits of the intended use of a particular drug outweigh the associated risks for that use. This process protects the public by ensuring that adequate scientific studies have been performed to provide a rational basis from which to conclude that the benefits of a drug outweighs its risks and by assuring that the product is accompanied by sufficient information to the physician and patient to permit its accurate prescription and use. Allowing any drug to bypass the federal approval process does a grave disservice to the public. Further, allowing any potential medication to bypass this process establishes a loophole that threatens to undermine the imperative for rigorous science as the basis for determining what constitutes good medicine.

C. Marijuana Remains a Controlled Substance

Marijuana has not been approved by the FDA to treat any disease or condition. Because marijuana has a high potential for abuse and no currently accepted medical use in the United States, it remains a Schedule I drug under the provisions of the Controlled Substance Act, Title II of the

Comprehensive Drug Abuse Prevention and Control Act of 1970. More-over, the FDA, as reported by Associate Commissioner for Health Affairs Dr. Stuart Nightingale, has not been provided sufficient studies on smoked marijuana to permit the agency to determine if the potential benefits of smoking marijuana for specific indications outweigh the known risks associated with the drug. Absent sufficient scientific evidence, there is no rational basis for a change in the classification of marijuana. It is in the interest of every American to ensure the continued application of the medical-scientific process to determine the safety and efficacy of drugs for therapeutic uses.

Absent sufficient scientific evidence, there is no rational basis for a change in the classification of marijuana.

D. No Rational Basis Exists for Exempting Marijuana From the Standard Approval Process—Anecdotes Should Not Drive Public Health Policy
We must ensure that all patients receive compassionate treatment using medicines proven to be safe and effective. However, the tragic lessons of history serve to remind us that hope and hearsay are not enough. Drug legalization proponents play on the sympathies all Americans share for those suffering from serious illnesses. We must do all that we can to minimize human suffering and to treat these tragic diseases. However, anecdotal claims about the medical benefits of smoked marijuana are insufficient grounds to subvert the protections Americans rely upon and deserve. In short, science provides no reason to exempt smoked marijuana from meeting the same rigorous standards required by all substances purporting to yield medical benefit.
1. Smoked Marijuana Poses Risks for the Individual User
The preponderance of scientific evidence to date demonstrates that marijuana is a dangerous drug. Marijuana is a contributing cause in the injury and death to users and non-users alike. Research shows that smoked marijuana, in addition to impairing normal brain function, also damages the heart, lungs, reproductive and immune systems. Recent studies show that regular, heavy marijuana use compromises the ability to learn and remember information primarily by impairing an individual's ability to focus, sustain, and shift attention. . . . Compared to the normal slides, the brain slides of the marijuana abuser clearly show diminished activity in all cross sections, particularly in the cerebellum. Lower cerebellar metabolism explains not only defects in motor coordination, but also seems to account for some of the reported learning disturbances found in chronic marijuana users. These effects are alarming among adults; they are extremely dangerous for adolescents.
2. Smoked Marijuana is a Significant Risk to America's 68 Million Children
Medical marijuana initiatives present even greater risks to our young people. Drug use, in particular marijuana use, among our young people is already too high. The rate of drug use among our children is linked to their perceptions of risks related to drugs. Referenda that tell our children that marijuana is a "medicine" send them the wrong signal about the

dangers of illegal drugs—increasing the likelihood that more children will turn to drugs. Moreover, marijuana is a "gateway" drug, leading children into more harmful drug use and eventually addictions.

a. Drug Use is Up Among Young People

The results from the National Household Survey on Drug Abuse (NHSDA) over the past few years suggest that the general decline in drug use from the peak of the late 1970s may have ended. No significant changes—either up or down—in illicit drug use or in the total numbers of casual and hardcore users were reported in 1996, compared with 1992, 1993, 1994, or 1995. Current drug use appears to have stabilized at about 6 percent of the general population. However, illicit drug use by adolescents has been increasing steadily since 1992.

The rate of current drug use of any illicit drug among youth ages 12 to 17 was 10.9 percent in 1995. Although that figure dropped to 9 percent in 1996, the rate remains markedly higher over 1992's low of 5.3 percent. Marijuana represents the bulk of this increase in drug abuse among children. According to the 1996 NHSDA, the rate of past-month marijuana use among children ages 12 to 17 was 7.1 percent, more than double the 3.4 percent long-term low for 1992. The consequences of youth marijuana use are devastating; over half (55 percent) of all youths ages 15-17 admitted to drug treatment, were seeking treatment for marijuana. (SAMHSA Office of Applied Studies.)

The 1997 *Back to School Survey* conducted by the Center on Addiction and Substance Abuse (CASA) at Columbia University also found that drug use is becoming more commonplace for our young people. The study found that an increasing number of children had been exposed to: deaths from substance abuse-related incidents, kids coming to school drunk or high, smoking, drinking and drug sales on school grounds, students expelled or suspended for possessing, using or selling drugs, and parties where marijuana is available. The study further found that teens are more likely to see drugs sold at school than in the neighborhood—41 percent of high school students have seen drugs sold at their schools, while only 25 percent have seen them sold in their neighborhoods. The 1997 CASA study also found that 74 percent of high school students and 52 percent of middle school students say a student has been expelled or suspended for possessing, using, or selling drugs in the past year. 56 percent of high school students and 24 percent of middle school students have attended a party in the past six months where marijuana was available.

b. Attitudes Determine Behaviors

The University of Michigan's annual *Monitoring The Future* (MTF) survey of drug use among youth, the preeminent report on juvenile attitudes and drug use rates, shows that as our children become more accepting of drug use and less fearful of its consequences, they increasingly use marijuana and other drugs of abuse.

- According to the MTF Survey, youth attitudes about drugs began to soften in 1989. These changes were reflected by lowered rates of disapproval and diminished perceptions of drug use as risky. Two years later, marijuana use by our children began to increase. The MTF reports that marijuana use among 8th graders was 3.2 percent in 1991, and increased each year thereafter to a rate of 11.3 percent in 1996.

- The MTF also reports that the rate of marijuana use among 10th and 12th graders began to increase in 1992. Twelfth graders' use increased from 11.9 percent in 1992 to 21.9 percent by 1996; 10th grade use increased from 8.1 percent in 1992 to 20.4 percent by 1996.

Dr. Lloyd Johnston, who has directed the MTF survey since the 1970s, suggests "generational forgetting" as a major factor contributing to the five-year trend (1991-1996) of increased drug use among our children. His theory holds that as new generations have less direct experience with the negative consequences of drug use, the likelihood that they will begin using drugs increases. Dr. David Musto of Yale University has also documented this phenomenon of learned experience informing decisions to use drugs since the turn of the century. Clearly, when people see firsthand the pernicious effects of illegal drugs, they tend to reject them. This may be one of the reasons past-month marijuana usage rates declined from 10.9 percent to 9 percent in 1996 among those ages 12 to 17 (NHSDA).

Changing youth attitudes toward marijuana and other drugs is the key to reducing drug use among our children. We cannot afford any further erosion of youth attitudes towards drugs by allowing marijuana to be falsely depicted as a safe and effective medicine. When Americans think of smoking marijuana, erroneously the image they remember is "Cheech and Chong." Whether intended or not, permitting the "medical" use of smoked marijuana will send the false and powerful message to our adolescents that marijuana use is beneficial. If pot is medicine, teenagers rightfully will reason, how can it hurt you? At a time when we need to be reaching out to our young people and explaining the dangers of drug use, we can ill afford to send our children a mixed—or more accurately a mixed up—message on marijuana. No one should make the mistake of believing that increased societal acceptance of marijuana will not cause drug abuse to increase among our children.

The preponderance of scientific evidence to date demonstrates that marijuana is a dangerous drug.

---

c. Marijuana is a "Gateway" Drug

The danger of sending the wrong message to our children about marijuana is compounded by the fact that smoking marijuana can often be the first step down a slippery path that leads to the use of drugs like cocaine, heroin, LSD, and methamphetamine. Most young people who smoke marijuana do not end up addicted to drugs. However, NHSDA reports and research by the Center on Addiction and Substance Abuse at Columbia University (CASA) both establish a strong correlation between marijuana use and cocaine use. Among those young people who have tried cocaine, virtually all used marijuana first.

CASA's October 1994 report on *Cigarettes, Alcohol, Marijuana: Gateways to Illicit Drug Use*, concluded that a 12 to 17-year old who uses marijuana is 85 times more likely to use cocaine than one who does not. This statistical correlation is 8 times stronger than the link between smoking and lung cancer, 17 times stronger than the link between exposure to asbestos and lung cancer and, 20 times stronger than that between high cholesterol and heart disease. The report also found that the earlier children begin to smoke marijuana, the more likely they are to subsequently use cocaine. Sixty percent of children who used marijuana before the age of 15 progressed to cocaine use, while only 20 percent of those who began smoking marijuana after the age of 17 did so.

These strong statistical correlations should inform both individual behavior and public policy. Parents, mentors, and children should conclude that smoking marijuana is not innocuous. All of us should understand that anything that directly or indirectly causes increased marijuana use by our children also paves the way for increased "hard" drug use and addiction.

We cannot afford any further erosion of youth attitudes towards drugs by allowing marijuana to be falsely depicted as a safe and effective medicine.

---

3. Drug Availability Leads to More Abuse and Addiction
Allowing the medical use of smoked marijuana would also likely increase the availability of marijuana, thereby increasing the risks of widespread drug use. As drugs become more available, abuse and addiction rise. By allowing marijuana to be legally grown, and used, medical marijuana initiatives are likely to increase the amount of marijuana that is available on our streets and in our schools for illegal use. The burgeoning number of cannabis clubs creates a huge potential for diversion to the streets, where teenagers comprise a lucrative target market. The potential for black market spillover is heightened because the referenda that are at issue provide little or no effective medical or law enforcement supervision of the use of marijuana. For example:

- California Proposition 215 fails to define both what constitutes a "caregiver" and the "conditions" for which marijuana could be used. Given that some advocates claim marijuana can be used to help everything from writer's cramp to diarrhea, virtually anyone possessing marijuana could claim some "caregivers" relationship to someone with some form of "condition." Because 215 contains no age limitation, a child could legally use marijuana on a verbal—or even Internet—recommendation of any physician, even without an examination.
- District of Columbia initiative, "Measure 57," provides that up to 20 people would be allowed to cultivate and sell unlimited quantities of marijuana for an individual with a condition drawn from a similarly amorphous range of conditions. If this initiative were to become law, drug traffickers would be basically shielded from successful prosecution. [Supporters failed to gather enough signatures to place the measure on the ballot for 1997.]

The law of supply and demand suggests that increasing the supply of marijuana available in the United States will cause the price of marijuana to drop even more and the psychoactive properties of the drug to further increase.

4. Science Documents the Risks of Marijuana Use to Individuals and Society

For decades, U.S. policy-makers have opposed the legalization of marijuana based on the weight of the available scientific evidence. Marijuana advocates have mounted a well-financed and sophisticated public relations campaign to persuade Americans of their point of view. These deceptive public relations efforts have relied almost exclusively on personal anecdotes to support their position. Anecdotes aside, the scientific data currently available paint a strikingly different picture from the image those who support legalization would have the American public see.

For example, two recent research studies, published in June 1997 in *Science*, have demonstrated disturbing similarities between marijuana's effects on the brain and those produced by highly addictive drugs like cocaine, heroin, alcohol, and nicotine. According to David Friedman, M.D., a neurobiologist at Bowman Gray School of Medicine, these studies "send a powerful message that should raise everyone's awareness about the dangers of marijuana use."

Meanwhile, misconceptions about marijuana continue to abound. Confused by conflicting messages, it is no wonder that many Americans, especially our youth, do not understand what current scientific research is teaching us about the damaging effects of smoked marijuana. Current research points to serious risks for society. Marijuana smoke contains cancer-causing compounds, reduces workplace productivity, and is increasingly prevalent in automobile accidents and youth fatalities. Examples of recent findings include:

- A roadside study, conducted in Memphis, Tennessee, of reckless drivers not believed to be impaired by alcohol, found that 45 percent tested positive for marijuana. (Brookoff D et al., *Testing Reckless Drivers for Cocaine and Marijuana*, New Eng J Med 320:762-768, 1994.)
- Marijuana impairs coordination, perception, and judgment, causing many accidents. A study of 1,023 trauma victims revealed that marijuana had been used by 34.7 percent. (Soderstrom CA et al., *Marijuana and Alcohol Use Among 1,023 Trauma Patients*, Archives of Surg 123:733-737, 1988.)
- One study conducted at the R Adams Cowley Shock Trauma Center, University of Maryland Medical Center, Baltimore, found that 34 (32.1 percent) of the 106 motorcyclists treated for injuries tested positive for marijuana. (Soderstrom CA et al., *Psychoactive Substance Use Disorders Among Seriously Injured Trauma Center Patients*, JAMA. 277 (22): 1769-74, 1997 June 11.)
- A study of 182 fatal truck accidents revealed that 12.5 percent of the drivers had used marijuana, in comparison to 12.5 percent for alcohol, 8.5 percent for cocaine, 7.9 percent for stimulants. (Department of Transportation. National Transportation Safety Board Report, Washington, D.C., February 5, 1990.)
- The most consistent finding from the literature on employee marijuana use is its association with increased absenteeism. It is also associated with increased accidents, higher turnover, low job satisfaction, counterproductive behavior, withdrawal and antagonistic behavior, and higher use of employee assistance programs and medical benefits. (NIDA National Conference on Marijuana Use: Prevention, Treatment and Research, 1995.)

- Treatment figures show that 141,000 Americans were admitted in 1995 to drug treatment programs for marijuana addiction. Over half (55 percent) of all youths ages 15-17 admitted to drug treatment, were seeking treatment for marijuana. (SAMHSA Office of Applied Studies.)

II. Safeguarding the Public Health
A. ONDCP's Efforts to Inform Decision-makers and the Public

In order to preserve the protections enjoyed by our citizens, ONDCP will continue to provide assistance to state legislatures and urge them to support the federal response based on science. Our efforts to date include the widespread dissemination of the *ONDCP Policy Statements on Marijuana for Medical Purposes* and on *Industrial Hemp*. These policy statements have been sent to the governors of all the states, law enforcement agencies, and numerous nongovernmental organizations. . . . In addition, ONDCP has also focused further efforts to inform the public and decision-makers as to the dangers of medical marijuana referenda in those states where such initiatives are under strong consideration. . . .

Medical marijuana initiatives are likely to increase the amount of marijuana that is available . . . for illegal use.

B. ONDCP's Efforts Demonstrate the Federal Commitment to Science Over Ideology
1. Scientific Studies

The efforts of the Department of Health and Human Services and ONDCP demonstrate the federal government's commitment to and reliance upon the scientific process as the appropriate means to determine the potential medical use, if any, for smoked marijuana. To that end, we have supported the following actions:

- *Institute of Medicine (IOM) Study:* In January 1997, ONDCP commissioned the IOM of the National Academy of Science (NAS) to conduct a comprehensive review of the known health effects and potential medical use of smoked marijuana. This evaluation is now assessing the current state of scientific knowledge; identify gaps in the knowledge base about marijuana; and will include clinical, medical, and scientific evidence on the following topics:
  - the neurological mechanism of action of marijuana;
  - the effects of marijuana on health and behavior;
  - marijuana's possible "gateway" characteristics;
  - the efficacy of therapeutic use of marijuana for specific medical conditions; and,
  - the effects of marijuana use compared with approved alternative psychotherapies.

The IOM has selected two "Principal Investigators" to conduct the study. These Investigators will now solicit additional expertise from universities, health professional schools, medical centers, hospices, state and local health departments, and other resources as appropriate. There will be three public meetings, at least one will be held on each coast, to foster maximum input. The final report will be released to the public upon completion in December 1998. We look forward to sharing these results with the subcommittee and the other members of Congress as they become available.

• *The National Institutes of Health (NIH) Workshop on Medical Utility of Marijuana:* In February, 1997, the NIH convened a 2-day meeting to review the scientific data concerning the potential therapeutic uses for marijuana and the need for and feasibility of additional research. The Ad Hoc Group of Experts received testimony from recognized experts in the field as well as public testimony. In August 1997, this group of experts released their report to the NIH. . . .

The panel concluded that the risks associated with marijuana, especially smoked marijuana, must be considered not only in terms of immediate adverse effects on the lungs, but also the long-term effects in patients with chronic diseases. The experts also were concerned about the possibility that frequent and prolonged marijuana use might lead to clinically significant impairments of immune system function is great enough that studies on immune function should be part of any research project on the medical uses of marijuana. This is especially true in studies involving patients with compromised immune systems. Members of the group also were concerned about the effects of the dangerous combustion byproducts of smoked marijuana on patients with chronic diseases. Based on these risks, they favored the development of a smoke-free inhaled delivery system that could provide to the patient purer forms of marijuana's most active ingredient, delta-9-tetrahydrocannabinol (THC), or its related compounds known as cannabinoids.

According to Dr. Harold Varmus, the NIH is open to receiving research grant applications for studies of the medical efficacy of marijuana. Applications will undergo the normal scientific review process. NIH is prepared to fund applications that meet the accepted standards of scientific design and that, on the basis of peer review, are competitive with other applications that qualify for funding.

Misconceptions about marijuana continue to abound.

• *Development of Alternative Delivery Systems for THC:* THC, the major psychoactive ingredient in the marijuana plant, is already available as a synthetic FDA-approved medication known as "Marinol," which is taken by mouth. Like all drugs authorized by the FDA, Marinol has proved itself safe and effective in valid clinical trials for the control of nausea and for wasting due to AIDS. THC has not been shown to be safe and effective for any other condition. Like almost all drugs used in modern medicine—for reasons of quality control and safety—THC is a pure substance, not a crude and variable mixture in a plant.

ONDCP has met with pharmaceutical representatives to determine their time-table for the development of alternative delivery systems such as inhalers, skin patches, and/or suppositories. Development of these alternative delivery systems over the next 2-5 years will provide a safer means of delivering THC. Efforts are now underway to educate physicians regarding the efficacy and availability of Marinol as well as proper dosing strategies to achieve maximum therapeutic effect.

How many individuals truly are unable to obtain relief with . . . existing FDA-approved medications?

---

2. Recent Advances Have Increased the Availability of Effective Medications
In addition to the scientific efforts being undertaken by the government, medical research in general is increasing the availability of other effective treatments that stand to render any potential need for medical marijuana as obsolete. Philip Kanof, M.D., Ph.D., a distinguished psychiatrist and pharmacologist at the VA Medical Center in Tucson, raises an important question: How many individuals truly are unable to obtain relief with appropriate use of existing FDA-approved medications? According to Dr. Kanof, newer 5HT3 receptor antagonists such as odansetron and granisetron have been very successful in managing nausea and vomiting in most chemotherapy patients. Drugs such as baclofen, benzodiazepines, and the newly approved tizanidine often produce significant relief from spasticity due to multiple sclerosis. And, as previously mentioned, Marinol is often effective in stimulating appetite in those AIDS patients suffering from a wasting syndrome.

To the extent that patients are suffering, it is important to question the degree to which their suffering is caused by their inability to obtain relief from existing medications, or because their physicians may not be as well informed as they might be about existing therapeutic options. Dr. Kanof urges that the first step towards alleviating the suffering of these patients should be the dissemination of algorithms for appropriate pharmacological management of these conditions—not encouraging the use of a carcinogenic drug with no accepted medical uses and significant abuse potential.

C. ONDCP is Working to Change Perceptions of Drug Use Among Our Nation's Youth
Regardless of whether smoked marijuana eventually demonstrates scientific merit for medical use, the number one goal of the *National Drug Control Strategy* remains that of educating and enabling youth to reject illegal drugs. ONDCP has developed a clear and powerful objective to meet that goal: the proposed Anti-drug Abuse Youth-Oriented Media Campaign. We recognize the tremendous power of the media in driving public opinion. Young people are particularly susceptible to the influences of television, the Internet and radio. Unfortunately, in recent years the number of drug-related public service announcements (PSAs) carried by television, radio, and print media have decreased markedly.

At the same time, there has been an increase in music, TV, movies, Internet web sites, fashion, humor, and other forms of communication that normalize or glamorize illegal drugs. Advertising experts believe targeted, high-impact paid media ads are the most cost-effective, quickest means of changing patterns of drug-use behavior by altering adolescent perceptions of danger and social disapproval of drugs. It is also the most effective means of reaching baby-boomer parents who may be ambivalent about sending strong anti-drug messages to their kids.

America needs to reverse the trends of youth drug use and diminishing PSAs by developing a public education campaign that supplements anti-drug announcements already offered by dedicated organizations like the Partnership for a Drug-Free America and the National Center for Advancement and Prevention. Youth will be warned about the hazards of illegal drugs and shown the advantages of a drug-free lifestyle. Information-based material will be repeated with sufficient frequency to reinforce learning and motivate youth to reject illegal drugs.

III. A Shared Commitment

Addressing the problem of drug use in America will only be possible through a shared commitment to progress. The bipartisan support of Congress has been instrumental to the work of the Office of National Drug Control Policy. We welcome and look forward to your continued help on a range of initiatives, including, but not limited to:

- Passage of ONDCP's reauthorization;
- Protection of the time-proven system that shields Americans from bad medicine;
- Approval of the Anti-drug Youth-Oriented Media Campaign; and,
- Assistance with restoring the Administration's budget request in drug-related areas, particularly with respect to the Safe and Drug Free Schools Program.

Your support for these and other initiatives is vital to continued progress in decreasing the use of illegal drugs in America.

Thank you for this opportunity to testify on the issue of medical marijuana referenda in America. ONDCP remains committed to addressing this issue on the basis of sound science. The American public has the right to expect that our medicines are both safe and effective. It is our job—Congress and the Administration working together—to protect our citizens, in particular America's children. We look forward to a continued bipartisan effort to uphold the highest standards of American medicine while ensuring that our youth are equally protected.

9

Additional Research on Medical Marijuana Is Warranted

Marc A. Schuckit

Marc A. Schuckit is a professor of psychiatry at the University of California School of Medicine and director of the Alcoholism Research Center in San Diego Veterans Administration Hospital. He edits the Drug Abuse and Alcoholism Newsletter *published by the Vista Hill Foundation, a nonprofit mental health care organization.*

Marijuana has been used for many years to stimulate appetite, to prevent nausea, to treat glaucoma, and for other medical uses. Marinol, a synthetic form of THC, marijuana's primary active ingredient, is legally available in pill form. In part because marijuana is classified as a Schedule I drug and cannot be prescribed by doctors, insufficient research exists to determine whether smoked marijuana has medical advantages over legal medicines, including Marinol. Because marijuana does possess potential medical properties, and because some patients do not respond well to existing treatments, further research on marijuana should be pursued.

The active ingredient of marijuana, a product of the Cannabis sativa plant, is delta-9-tetrahydrocannabinol or THC. Potential medical uses for this drug have been cited for perhaps 5,000 years. During the 1800s there were numerous papers on the therapeutic use of marijuana for indications that included stimulation of appetite, muscle relaxation, analgesia, and for the treatment of migraines, convulsions, and sleep disorders. Extracts of marijuana were listed in the *Pharmacopoeia,* a guideline for clinicians.

With the turn of the century, a number of events combined to first decrease the number of studies of the medicinal use of marijuana substances, and then obliterate any possibility of their prescription. First, in the early 1900s alternative pharmacological treatments were found for many of the indications of marijuana. The newer drugs could be orally in-

Reprinted from Marc A. Schuckit, "Does Marijuana Have Any Medical Value?" *Drug Abuse & Alcoholism Newsletter* (Vista Hill Foundation), April 1996, by permission of the author.

gested, were more consistent in potency, and had less erratic absorption and therapeutic responses.

Subsequently, legal impediments for the medical use of marijuana appeared in 1937 with the passing of the Marijuana Tax Act, which effectively removed THC-containing drugs from the therapeutic armamentarium. Then, the 1970 Uniform Controlled Substances Act listed marijuana as a Schedule I drug, indicating a substance with a high potential for abuse, lacking acceptable medical indications, and considered unsafe even for use under medical supervision. In 1972, the National Organization for the Reform of Marijuana Laws (NORML) took steps to have marijuana changed from Schedule I to Schedule II, a move which would allow for legal prescription of this agent. While supported by several additional groups, including some physicians' associations, public hearings were not scheduled until the mid 1980s. In 1988, a Drug Enforcement Administration judge ruled that it would be appropriate to use this drug under medical supervision, but the potential move to Schedule II was overruled in 1989, a step that was finalized in early 1992.

There is little argument against the contention that marijuana causes a decrease in nausea and vomiting in chemotherapy patients.

In a commentary in the *Journal of the American Medical Association* in 1995, Lester Grinspoon and James Bakalar reviewed much of this history and offered a "plea for reconsideration" regarding the medical prescription of marijuana. This letter was based on their 1993 book entitled *Marijuana, the Forbidden Medicine*. This viewpoint reviews the available information regarding the potential medical usefulness of marijuana.

Before describing specific medical uses, a brief review of some pharmacological information might be helpful. Several synthetic cannabinoids have been developed. Pure delta-9-THC is supposedly available "on the street," but is unlikely to actually be the sole component of anything purchased as THC. Rather, a variety of other substances or fillers are most likely to be involved. Currently, there is one pharmacological form of THC available by prescription, which is marketed as an antiemetic and appetite stimulant. This substance, dronabinol (Marinol), consists of delta-9-THC suspended in sesame oil in gelatin capsules. The following discussion regarding the medicinal importance of marijuana must therefore consider not only whether the marijuana itself is of value, but also whether the presently available prescribed cannabinoid is sufficient to treat the conditions for which it might be used.

The control of nausea and vomiting

There is little argument against the contention that marijuana causes a decrease in nausea and vomiting in chemotherapy patients. Reports of marijuana's effectiveness in this regard contributed to the 1985 decision by the FDA to approve the medicinal form of THC, Marinol. THC is potentially important because the vomiting and "dry heaves" in the course of chemotherapy can last for hours or days, and can be followed by additional days or weeks of nausea. These unpleasant side effects can contribute to the weight loss experienced by cancer patients. Also, in more rare instances, violent episodes of vomiting can cause a patient to crack a rib, or even suffer a life-threatening tear to the food tube or esophagus. This severe and debilitating nausea and vomiting add to the apprehension with which cancer patients view all subsequent treatments, and can contribute to either lowering the dose of the anticancer drug or even stopping the treatments altogether.

Many clinicians feel that smoked marijuana produces a significant benefit above that observed with synthetic THC.

For several decades the anti-nausea drug prochlorperazine (Compazine) has been helpful, but not fully effective. In the 1990s a new agent with fewer side effects and greater efficacy, ondansetron (Zofran), was marketed. However, in cases where these agents are not sufficient to control symptoms, Marinol can be important. Unfortunately, this drug is difficult to use when patients are unable to keep any foods or liquids down, and the absorption is relatively slow and erratic.

In light of these problems, a 1990 survey by R.E. Doblin and M.A.R. Kleiman evaluated whether smoked marijuana might have some advantages over Marinol. Sent to 2,430 oncologists and generating a reply from 43%, the questionnaire addressed several issues. First, 70% of the oncologists noted that one or more of their patients had ever used marijuana as an antiemetic in the course of chemotherapy. Of the physicians expressing an opinion, almost two-thirds reported that marijuana had been effective in 50% or more of their patients, while only 56% reported the same of the synthetic agent. The physicians also reported that Marinol was somewhat more likely than marijuana to result in unpleasant side effects. Furthermore, 44% of the oncologists admitted they had suggested that a patient obtain marijuana illegally in order to alleviate their nausea and vomiting. Finally, 54% of the respondents felt that marijuana should be placed as a Schedule II drug, and 48% said that they would prescribe it if it were legal.

Thus, at least for use in chemotherapy, many clinicians feel that smoked marijuana produces a significant benefit above that observed with synthetic THC. Perhaps because it is absorbed through the lungs, THC levels from marijuana might be more reliable than with Marinol. It is also easier for a patient to titrate the effective dose with a minimum of side effects, and to tolerate administering the drug despite severe nausea. Finally, some clinicians suggest that there might be other components to the marijuana smoke, not just THC, that are of help.

The treatment of glaucoma

The normal shape and optimal functioning of the eye depend upon a delicate balance between the amount of fluid produced in the eye (aqueous humor) and the amount of this substance that flows out through channels. If either too much fluid is produced or the outlet blocked, the pressure in the eye increases and can produce severe damage to the optic nerve. This increase in pressure, or glaucoma, is observed in 1.5% of the population age 50 and over, including 5% of those over the age of 70. It is one of the leading causes of blindness in the United States.

There are a number of relatively effective ways to treat glaucoma. First, drugs that block the actions of adrenalin, including a group of medications called beta-blockers, enhance the flow of fluid out of the eye. However, these drugs have side effects that include fatigue, depression, and an increase in breathing problems. Eye drops with pilocarpine can also be helpful, as can pills containing a carbonic anhydrase inhibitor which decreases the production of the aqueous humor. These pills, however, can be associated with symptoms of nausea, headaches, and a decreased appetite.

There are few, if any, appropriate double-blind controlled trials of the use of marijuana in the treatment of AIDS.

In about 1970, it was discovered that smoking marijuana is associated with a number of changes in the eye including a significant decrease in the pressure. This was subsequently tested in patients with glaucoma, and discovered to last for four to five hours, with no evidence that repeated smoking produced tolerance to the effect. At least in animals, the action appeared to be observed with marijuana-containing eye drops, not just smoking.

The book by Grinspoon and Bakalar presents case histories of patients with severe glaucoma who were either unresponsive to the more usual treatments, or who could not tolerate the side effects. For these individuals, it appears as if marijuana contributed to saving sight. However, more data are needed regarding the possibility that a synthetic THC preparation in eye drops might be helpful in severe glaucoma, or if smoking of the marijuana itself is required.

Appetite stimulation

A textbook description of the effects of smoking marijuana is likely to highlight the "munchies." Indeed, the effect that marijuana products have on hunger and subsequent consumption of foods has been well documented in both human and animal research.

There are few appetite stimulants available for clinical use. Some of the antidepressant medications, such as amitriptyline (Elavil), are associated with weight gain. However, these medications have side effects, and have not been extensively tested for disorders in which weight loss is prominent.

High on the list of such "wasting" conditions is the acquired immunodeficiency syndrome or AIDS. A prominent symptom of this syndrome, also called "slim disease" in Africa, is a loss of appetite. There are numerous anecdotal reports of the effects of marijuana in AIDS patients. At least subjectively, patients are likely to report both an increase in feelings of hunger and in the pleasure of eating.

Unfortunately, perhaps as a reflection of some of the restrictive laws regarding the use of a Schedule I drug, there are few, if any, appropriate double-blind controlled trials of the use of marijuana in the treatment of AIDS. Nor is there an extensive literature on the use of synthetic THC in this condition. These substances might also be helpful in people with terminal cancer who have lost their appetites.

Muscle relaxation

One severe and painful consequence of some injuries to the spinal cord, especially if there is subsequent paralysis, is muscle spasm. The loss of healthy nerve functions between the spinal cord and the muscles not only produces an inability to initiate voluntary movement, but also causes violent and painful involuntary muscle constrictions.

There are a number of muscle relaxants that can be of help. However, at least anecdotally, many patients with paraplegia and quadriplegia find that the existing treatments are not potent enough. The Grinspoon and Bakalar book cites a number of case reports supporting the efficacy of marijuana in these patients, as well as at least one more scientific survey. The latter indicated that 50% or more of individuals with severe spinal cord injury used marijuana in an attempt to control spasms. Also, a 1990 study by three Swiss neurologists reported that oral THC caused a marked reduction in muscle spasms in the paraplegic patient they treated.

Thus, THC appears appropriate for further testing for this condition. The present data do not make it clear whether marijuana itself is essential, or if the synthetic form of THC currently available by prescription would be sufficient.

Additional potential medical indications

There are also incomplete but suggestive data regarding the use of marijuana in the treatment of multiple sclerosis, seizures, migraines, chronic pain, and other medical disorders. However, because the data are fewer and in general speculative, these potential indications for marijuana are not discussed in more detail here. . . .

Potential dangers and benefits

Despite my background in pharmacology, I am very conservative about the use of medications. In order for me to prescribe a drug, I have to be convinced by data on effectiveness and safety.

In August of 1990 I reviewed some of the potential dangers of marijuana. These include impairment in driving ability, dangers to the lungs from marijuana tobacco smoke, and impairments in cognition and motivational drive that can linger for days after the last use.

On the other hand, this review has revealed potentially important medicinal effects of marijuana, and there are patients who either do not respond to or do not tolerate existing treatments. For some of these conditions, especially severe nausea and glaucoma, the dangers of marijuana do not appear to be significantly more than the potential problems associated with available legal drugs such as the barbiturates, benzodiazepines, and many of the medications marketed for appetite stimulation. The combination of effects, need, and modest level of dangers would seem to warrant additional research. However, because I am not a legal expert, it is difficult for me to say which steps are required to encourage further research with this substance. Keeping marijuana as a restricted drug, but moving it to Schedule II, would certainly appear to facilitate that goal.

10

Government Policy Discourages Important Research into Medical Marijuana

David M. Fine

David M. Fine is a production assistant and former assistant editor of The American Prospect, *a liberal public policy journal.*

There exists growing public and scientific support for more research on marijuana's possible medical uses and to allow doctors to prescribe marijuana for their patients. However, federal government officials, afraid of appearing soft on drugs, have effectively stymied scientific research on medical marijuana by turning down grant requests and restricting access to the drug. The government has also refused to reclassify marijuana to make it legally available by prescription. These policies create hardship for ill people who could perhaps benefit from the drug.

For several decades, researchers have sought to determine whether marijuana has legitimate medical uses, and narcotics control agencies have discouraged them from finding out. Now a new round of federally funded research may provide some answers—or will it? The latest skirmish between scientists and police comes on the heels of two popular 1996 referenda, in California and Arizona, legalizing the medical use of marijuana. But since it remains a federal crime to grow, sell, or prescribe cannabis, the referenda have created only a legal morass.

Barry McCaffrey, director of the White House Office of National Drug Control Policy, derided the propositions as "hoax referendums," and insisted that voters had been "duped" by deceitful ad campaigns whose real intent was to legalize drugs. Attorney General Janet Reno announced that prescribing or recommending marijuana was still a violation of federal law, and that any doctors who did so could be prosecuted and lose their

Reprinted from David M. Fine, "Grassroots Medicine," *The American Prospect*, vol. 34, September/October 1997, by permission of the author and *The American Prospect*. Copyright 1997 The American Prospect, PO Box 383080, Cambridge, MA 02138. All rights reserved.

license to prescribe all drugs regulated by the Drug Enforcement Administration (DEA).

However, the medical use of marijuana has been gaining respectability. Several states have research programs of their own and some governors, including Republican William Weld of Massachusetts, openly endorse medical legalization. The editor of the prestigious *New England Journal of Medicine*, Jerome Kassirer, lambasted the Clinton administration in an editorial entitled "Federal Foolishness and Marijuana" that received national attention. "To prohibit physicians from alleviating suffering by prescribing marijuana for seriously ill patients," Kassirer wrote, "is misguided, heavy-handed, and inhumane."

In January 1997, Director McCaffrey, finding himself knee-deep in a debate in which he was little qualified to participate, tried to defuse criticism with an announcement that the Institute of Medicine (IOM) would be given $1 million to conduct an 18-month review of the current literature on marijuana. Later that month Harold Varmus, director of the National Institutes of Health (NIH), announced that the NIH would convene a workshop on the medical utility of marijuana. "We have no rationale for not looking into it," Dr. Varmus said in a phone interview.

But the IOM conducted a similar study back in 1982 and issued a report entitled "Marijuana and Health," concluding that "Marijuana and its derivatives or analogues might be useful in the treatment of glaucoma, of nausea and vomiting brought on by cancer chemotherapy, and of asthma. . . ." A review of the existing literature, as Kassirer pointed out, will likely be inconclusive because no definitive study has been done. The new IOM review, Kassirer said in an interview, "was a political maneuver designed to move the debate off center stage—it probably could be done in 18 days.". . .

The medical marijuana movement

Ever since the 1930s and the era of "Reefer Madness," when marijuana acquired both a countercultural stigma and allure, the federal government has resisted attempts to legalize marijuana for medical purposes—both by inhibiting research and by restricting access to the drug. The government has been fearful of sending the message that if marijuana is medically useful, it also can be used safely as a recreational drug. The scientific issue is unresolved, but nonetheless closed.

The medical marijuana movement emerged with the rise of recreational marijuana use in the 1960s. Marijuana had long been known to promote appetite, and a few studies in the first half of the twentieth century showed that it aided in alleviating nausea. Many chemotherapy patients found that smoking marijuana not only relieved their nausea and vomiting better than any of the legally available medications, but also enhanced appetite and relieved anxiety. For many, the relief from smoking pot was so strikingly better than from the use of Compazine, the antinauseant of choice, that word quickly spread among patients and doctors and then on to legislators.

In a 1980 congressional hearing titled "Health Consequences of Marijuana Abuse: Recent Findings and the Therapeutic Uses of Marijuana and the Use of Heroin to Reduce Pain," two prominent oncologists—Steven

Sallan, then clinical director of pediatric oncology at the Sidney Farber Cancer Institute, and Solomon Garb, president of the medical staff at the AMC Cancer Research Center in Lakewood, Colorado—and others attested to the medical utility of both smokable marijuana and its primary active ingredient, delta-9-THC. They also testified to the difficulties in obtaining the drugs to conduct research: While anyone could buy marijuana on the street on any given day, Garb had to wait seven months for his research supply and knew others who had waited up to two years.

The government has been fearful of sending the message that if marijuana is medically useful, it can also be used safely as a recreational drug.

However, marijuana remained a Schedule I drug—a substance with potential for abuse and no medical uses. Despite a number of petitions to move marijuana to Schedule II, the DEA refused even to hold a public hearing on the issue. So while the federal government resisted, states took the initiative. By the late 1980s, 34 states had passed some form of medical marijuana legislation. Several states organized marijuana research programs so they could legitimately obtain synthetic THC—and in a few cases, marijuana—from the federal government, for suffering patients. Results from studies, though not rigorously scientific, conducted in New Mexico, Tennessee, New York, and elsewhere, found that smokable marijuana and THC outperformed the best available prescription drugs, reporting success rates close to 90 percent; anecdotal evidence suggested that smoked marijuana was more effective than Marinol, the synthetic THC pill.

Finally, in 1985 the coalition of doctors, patients, and marijuana activists persuaded the Department of Health and Human Services to move Marinol to Schedule II, making it legally available by prescription to patients. Soon after, the DEA announced that public hearings on the rescheduling of marijuana itself would finally be held. Those hearings lasted two years and culminated in the recommendation of DEA Administrative Law Judge Francis L. Young in 1988, who wrote that

> it is unrealistic and unreasonable to require unanimity of opinion on the question confronting us. For the reasons there indicated, acceptance [of marijuana having a medical use] by a significant minority of doctors is all that can reasonably be required. This record makes it abundantly clear that such acceptance exists in the United States. . . . One must reasonably conclude that there is accepted safety for use of marijuana under medical supervision.

But the DEA administrator did not act on this recommendation and marijuana remained in Schedule I.

The pro-legalization National Organization for the Reform of Marijuana Laws (NORML) petitioned the DEA to reschedule marijuana for review again in 1992. Denying this petition, DEA Administrator Robert Bonner wrote in the *Federal Register*, "Our nation's top cancer experts reject marijuana for medical use." To support his claim, he cited the testimony of David S. Ettinger, a professor of medicine at Johns Hopkins University School of Medicine and "nationally respected cancer expert," who said: "There is no indication that marijuana is effective in treating nausea and vomiting resulting from radiation treatment or other causes. No legitimate studies have been conducted which make such conclusions."

Bonner thus concluded, "Not one nationally recognized cancer expert could be found to testify on marijuana's behalf." But in a phone interview, Ettinger said he had changed his position. He now believes that in cases of intractable nausea "smoking marijuana is reasonable" and that there are "patients for whom therapies don't work and in that situation anything is worth trying." He also said a study should be conducted comparing the efficacy of smoked marijuana to Marinol.

Closing the book on marijuana

From the late 1980s up to the present, the federal government has appeared content to close the book on the medical marijuana question, inhibiting any attempts at further research of its medical utility, and limiting research to marijuana's negative effects. In 1994 Dr. Donald Abrams, a California AIDS specialist, submitted a research proposal to compare smokable marijuana and Marinol because, he said, "we have 1,100 AIDS patients in the Bay Area using marijuana [on their own]." Abrams's draft proposal did not pass peer review, but the FDA helped Abrams develop a revised proposal, which was approved by several California research committees and submitted in August 1994. After a delay of nine months, Abrams received a letter from Dr. Alan Leshner, director of the NIDA, turning down the proposal and leaving no room for further negotiation over revisions. "As an AIDS investigator who has worked closely with the National Institutes of Health and the U.S. Food and Drug Administration for the past 14 years of this epidemic, I must tell you that dealing with your institute has been the worst experience of my career!" Abrams replied.

Polls show broad support for medicalization. An ABC/Discovery Channel nationwide poll conducted in May found that 69 percent of respondents favored permitting doctors to prescribe marijuana. Now, after several years of relative quiet, states and local organizations are again pursuing the issue of medical marijuana. The California Medical Association backed a bill in May 1997 that would provide $6 million for researching the medical benefits of marijuana, and Americans for Medical Rights is gearing up to get medical marijuana ballots placed in a half dozen states for 1998. In addition to the California and Arizona referenda, the state governments of Massachusetts and Washington are creating programs to distribute marijuana to qualifying patients, though of course these programs are contingent on federal approval. In a sense, these could be test cases, signaling whether federal health officials will keep an open mind about the potential medical benefits of cannabis.

Raising the hurdle

In the past, the DEA argued that marijuana had no accepted medical use. Now the government has altered that argument subtly, raising the hurdle for a revision in its policy. Director McCaffrey, in testimony December 2, 1996, before the Senate Judiciary Committee, stated, "There is no scientifically sound evidence that smoked marijuana is *medically superior to currently available therapies* [emphasis added]."

The federal government has appeared content to close the book on the medical marijuana question.

There are, in fact, some new anti-nausea treatments that may provide relief comparable or superior to marijuana. For example, new anti-emetic drugs such as Ondansetron and Kytril (trade names), are administered to patients intravenously, and work well. But they are difficult to administer and are astronomically expensive. In tablet form, for outpatient chemotherapy, Kytril retails for around $86 for a daily two-milligram dose. Legal marijuana would cost just a few cents a dose. Moreover, it is not FDA policy to disallow one treatment simply because another, more expensive or elaborate one is available. Dr. Robert Temple, associate director for medical policy in the Center for Drug Evaluation and Research at the FDA, who also attended the NIH workshop, told the *New York Times*, "FDA approval does not require that any [new] drug be better than, or even as good as, an existing drug." Such an action would be equivalent to the FDA denying approval to, say, Pepcid, because Tagamet is a sufficient acid-blocking drug.

Other Schedule I drugs have been rescheduled because they provided relatively minor increased flexibility or improvement in treatment. LAAM (L-alpha-acetylmethodol), a drug now used with or in place of methadone to treat heroin addicts, was recently moved from Schedule I to II because it can be taken every other day compared to the required daily prescription of methadone. This allows recovering addicts to use the day in the middle for counseling.

Marijuana vs. Marinol

Many AIDS patients suffer from AIDS wasting syndrome, during which they are so sick they cannot eat. Chemo-therapy and radiation-treatment patients often suffer from extreme nausea and vomiting. All of these patients might be candidates for marijuana therapy, to promote appetite and relieve nausea and vomiting. Many patients smoke marijuana that they obtain illegally because they can control the dosage: The palliative effects occur about 45 minutes faster and the psychoactive effects go away more quickly than when the patients take Marinol. Ironically, the government approved Marinol in part because it seemed less "recreational" than smoked marijuana. But clinically, the psychoactive effects of Marinol characteristically last nearly eight hours, while those of a comparable dose of smoked marijuana generally last between two and four.

Moreover, for patients suffering from extreme nausea and vomiting, the Marinol pill is not practical because they may not be able to retain it. In the 1980 congressional hearing on marijuana, Dr. Steven Sallan testified to the benefits of smoking as a venue for ingesting anti-nausea medication:

There is no question in my mind that the oral route for an anti-emetic, a pill, is the absolute worst route for the patient who has a lot of anticipatory nausea and vomiting. . . . The smoke route is in some ways ideal. Certainly when we want a drug to be absolutely sure, general anesthesia, we put it on the face, they breathe it across their lungs, it's in their bloodstream immediately.

Dr. Lester Grinspoon, author of *Marihuana: The Forbidden Medicine*, says it may be possible to inhale only the therapeutically effective chemicals of marijuana and leave the tar and carcinogens behind. He attests that marijuana can be heated to a certain point at which the cannabinoids (the pharmacologically effective chemicals) are released, but the plant will not actually burn. "In the future, [patients] will be inhaling the vapors of marijuana," Grinspoon said, if the government allows the technology to be developed. In an April 1997 interview in the online magazine *Salon*, Dr. William Beaver, professor of pharmacology at Georgetown and chair of the NIH workshop, mentioned the possibility of developing such a delivery system. Currently, however, paraphernalia laws forbid the production or the sale of marijuana vaporizers.

A Trojan horse for legalization?

Is medical marijuana just a stalking horse? It's true that pro-legalization organizations such as NORML play an active role in the medical marijuana movement. Philanthropist George Soros and his Drug Policy Foundation, advocates of general decriminalization, have financially backed medical marijuana initiatives. A February 17, 1997, article in the *New Republic*, "The Return of Pot" by Hanna Rosin, also characterized the raison d'être of the medical marijuana movement as general legalization. "The truth about the marijuana movement is . . . blindingly obvious after a day in [Dennis] Peron's club. The movement is . . . primarily about legalization," Rosin wrote. While the movement "may feature billboards of the infirm . . . in the offices of its activists you are more likely to find a different poster, a stoner classic: *The Declaration of Independence and the Constitution Were Written on Hemp Paper.*"

Having spent decades branding marijuana a killer weed, the government is caught in its own rhetoric.

The reality is that the medical legalization coalition includes potheads, scientists, oncologists, patients, and social reformers. Bill Zimmerman, who coordinated California's pro-legalization Proposition 215, says, "Some people supporting medical marijuana initiatives are without question using it as an attempt to legalize marijuana. Other people are supporting marijuana policy changes out of a genuine concern for patients. It's a free country." And while Rosin paints a pretty bleak picture of the California marijuana scene—scrawny pot junkies with grimy teeth using excuses of migraine headaches to legitimately obtain their fix—she leaves out biographies of activists like conservative notable William F. Buckley, Jr., who found marijuana's medical illegality absurd when his sister preferred it to standard drugs in alleviating the negative affects of her chemotherapy. Ironically, it is marijuana's medical illegality that perpetuates the very cannabis clubs Rosin finds contemptible. Such clubs would largely disappear if marijuana were available by prescription.

One curious footnote to this controversy is that the federal government is currently dispensing smokable marijuana—to eight individuals. The Food and Drug Administration began the Single Patient Investigational New Drug Program (commonly know as compassionate IND) in the mid-1970s. Settling out of court in the case *Randall v. U.S.*, the federal government determined it would provide Robert Randall, who suffered from glaucoma, smokable marijuana legally. Fourteen people in all were admitted to the compassionate IND program before its suspension in 1990 and its closure in 1992. The FDA ended the program due to a deluge of applications—again, the government was worried about the public perception of liberally dispensing the drug. Nonetheless, eight people, beneficiaries of a grandfather clause, continue to receive federal marijuana to this day.

Concerns about recreational use

The strongest argument against prescribed marijuana remains the concern that it would remove whatever stigma marijuana retains and thus proliferate recreational usage. Joseph Califano, president of the National Center on Addiction and Substance Abuse (CASA), wrote in a *Washington Post* op-ed attacking medical legalization:

> Our children are at stake here. . . . A state has an enormous interest in protecting children from proposals likely to make drugs such as marijuana, heroin and LSD more acceptable and accessible.

But would making marijuana prescribable do either? The list of dangerous and addictive drugs currently prescribable by physicians is enormous and all of them are tightly controlled by the DEA. Although opiates have been abused for centuries, drugs such as codeine, morphine, and dilaudid are carefully regulated, widely prescribed, and relieve the suffering of millions. The use of cocaine has declined drastically from 5.7 million people in 1985 to 1.4 million in 1994, and the drug is a prescribable Schedule II controlled substance.

At the 1980 congressional hearing, North Carolina Congressman Stephen Neal, the chairman of the task force, responded to similar fears expressed by the NIDA spokesperson in the following testimony:

> I have two teenage children. . . . They are at the prime age for exposure to these drugs. . . . It seems to me, watching them and watching what our government has done over the years, that we have spread a good deal of misinformation . . . and that people, and young people in particular respond very positively to accurate information. . . . I really think that my own kids can understand the difference be-

tween a use of a drug for a particular illness and its recreational use. . . . It just doesn't seem reasonable to me we would have to sacrifice the potential for some good use of these drugs . . . it doesn't seem consistent. Not only that, but I think kids will see right through it.

However, for President Clinton and many other elected officials, the question is not so simple.

Trapped in drug war rhetoric

Having spent decades branding marijuana a killer weed, the government is caught in its own rhetoric. This administration, like previous ones, is fearful that if it softens on the issue of the medical use of marijuana, it risks being labeled soft on drugs. When President Clinton began cutting the drug war budget during his first term, he was soon confronted with harsh criticism from the right—William Bennett wrote in a 1995 congressional testimony, "The Clinton Administration suffers from moral torpor on this issue"—and with claims of increased marijuana use among teens. These factors led Clinton to announce the largest drug war budget ever for 1996. Again in 1997, the United States has appropriated $16 billion for the drug war budget.

It remains to be seen whether the federal government will have the courage to allow scientists to resolve the issue of marijuana's medical use in the face of pot's long-standing cultural stigma. But the government will not depress recreational marijuana use or make progress in the war on hard drugs by denouncing referenda, threatening prosecution of doctors, and blocking legitimate medical research. It will only make it more difficult for severely ill people to relieve their suffering.

11

Medical Marijuana Should Not Be Permitted

Robert L. Maginnis

Robert L. Maginnis, a retired army lieutenant colonel, is a policy analyst for the Family Research Council, a conservative research and educational organization.

The question of legalizing marijuana for medical use became a national issue following the passage of two state propositions in 1996. Marijuana proponents are attempting to win public support for full legalization of the drug by making appeals for "compassion" for the sick. A close analysis, however, reveals that most scientific and medical authorities reject marijuana as medicine. Allowing marijuana, an addictive substance, to be used as medicine would increase drug abuse and create social and law enforcement problems.

L egalizing marijuana for medicine deserves a thorough analysis. Advocates say it is a prudent and "compassionate" step for seriously ill patients but the real issue is the legalizing of now-illicit drugs.

On November 5, 1996, the issue of the medical use of marijuana rocketed to national attention via two state propositions. California's "Compassionate Use Act" passed with 56 percent of the vote and permits "seriously ill Californians" to grow, possess and use marijuana legally. The law also permits use for "any other illness for which marijuana provides relief." It protects from prosecution doctors who prescribe marijuana no matter the alleged illness, and the prescription can be either "written or oral." There is no age restriction.

Arizona's "Drug Medicalization, Prevention and Control Act" was packaged as a truth-in-sentencing and drug prevention measure. Buried within the proposition was a provision which allows a physician to prescribe controlled substances like marijuana, heroin, LSD and methamphetamine to "reduce the pain and suffering of the seriously ill and terminally ill."

On December 2, 1996, General Barry McCaffrey, Director, Office of

Reprinted from Robert L. Maginnis, "Medical Marijuana," *Family Research Council Insight*, 1997, by permission of the Family Research Council.

National Drug Control Policy, told the U.S. Senate Judiciary Committee, "The Office of National Drug Control Policy strongly opposes Arizona's Proposition 200 and California's Proposition 215. . . . They both violate the medical-scientific process by which safe and effective medicines are evaluated for use by the medical community. Both measures are actually a quasi-legalization of dangerous drugs. We believe these two measures are unwise and represent a threat to our congressionally approved National Drug Control policy."[1]

Why oppose marijuana as medicine?

Marijuana as medicine is widely rejected despite claims otherwise.

Numerous prestigious medical associations—such as the American Medical Association, the National Multiple Sclerosis Society, the American Glaucoma Society, the American Academy of Ophthalmology and the American Cancer Society—all have rejected the claim that marijuana has any demonstrated medical utility.[2]

A National Institute of Drug Abuse study, entitled "Therapeutic Uses of Cannabis," embodies an exhaustive review of the medical literature. It reveals that the majority of studies show little or no effectiveness of marijuana when used for medical purposes and when its effects are warranted. There are legally approved drugs on the market containing the active ingredient in marijuana.[3]

Their Case: Pro-marijuana forces argue that smoking crude marijuana helps AIDS wasting syndrome patients.[4] The syndrome is characterized by at least a 10 percent weight loss with chronic fever, weakness, or diarrhea in the absence of other related illnesses contributing to the weight loss.

The Facts: Science shows that smoking anything [tobacco or marijuana] doubles the probability of contracting full-blown AIDS for HIV-infected patients and according to the Drug Information Analysis Service, the "efficacy of dronabinol [synthetic THC, marijuana's psychoactive ingredient] in reversing the wasting process in AIDS patients is yet to be determined."[5]

The National Institute on Allergy and Infectious Diseases has identified two commercially available treatments for anorexia/cachexia in patients with AIDS, Megace (magastrol acetate) and Marinol. The Institute dismisses marijuana as an effective AIDS wasting drug by identifying four limitations: drug absorption via smoking may be "impractical or unacceptable;" marijuana includes "a complex mixture of over 400 compounds including polyaeromatic hydrocarbons which are carcinogenic;" marijuana is often contaminated with salmonella and fungal spores which compromise the immune system; and the mind altering effect may distress patients.[6]

Their Case: Pro-marijuana groups argue that smoking crude marijuana is "good medicine" for glaucoma patients.[7] Glaucoma is characterized as rising pressure on the optic nerve which can lead to blindness.

The Facts: The National Eye Institute (NEI) reports "there is no scientifically verifiable evidence that marijuana or its derivatives are safe and effective in the treatment of glaucoma." None of NEI's marijuana-based research studies demonstrate that THC can safely and effectively lower intraocular pressure enough to prevent optic nerve damage from glaucoma.[8]

Dr. George L. Spaeth, the first President of the American Glaucoma Society and Director of the Glaucoma Service at the internationally known Wills Eye Hospital in Philadelphia has "not found any documentary evidence which indicates that a single patient has had his or her natural history of the disease altered by smoking marijuana."[9]

Dr. Keith Green, Director of Ophthalmology Research at the Medical College of Georgia, states, "It is clear that there is no evidence that marijuana use prevents the progression of visual loss in glaucoma."[10]

Their Case: Marijuana-as-medicine proponents claim that crude pot helps alleviate nausea and vomiting associated with the effects of chemotherapy.[11]

The Facts: In 1996, Harmon J. Eyre, Executive Vice President for Research and Cancer Control for the American Cancer Society stated, there is "no reason to support the legalization of marijuana for medical use."[12]

Joanne Schellenbach, spokeswoman for the American Cancer Society, said her group feels there is "no need to treat the side effects of chemotherapy" with marijuana. There are ample legal pharmaceuticals available to do this which don't present the [medical] problems [caused by] inhaling," she said.[13]

Dr. David S. Ettinger, associate director of the Johns Hopkins Oncology Center, and a nationally respected cancer expert, has written that "There is no indication that marijuana is effective in treating nausea and vomiting resulting from radiation treatment. . . . No legitimate studies have been conducted which make such conclusions."[14]

Their Case: Marijuana proponents allege that crude pot can limit the muscle pain and spasticity associated with multiple sclerosis (MS).[15]

The Facts: A 1994 study published in *Clinical Pharmacology & Therapeutics* found that a single marijuana cigarette increased postural tracking error, decreased response speed and further impaired posture and balance. The authors concluded that marijuana smoking impairs coordination and balance in patients with spastic MS.[16]

In 1994, the National Institute of Neurological Disorders and Stroke stated, "There is no evidence that marijuana is effective in modifying the course of MS." The Institute also found that "Marijuana is problematic as a therapy for MS" because "There is no standardized product and method of assuring the bioavailability of its ingredients."[17]

Numerous prestigious medical associations . . . have rejected the claim that marijuana has any demonstrated medical utility.

The propositions to legalize marijuana as medicine undermine safe medical procedures.

The Food and Drug Administration (FDA) has a rigorous scientific process for regulating drugs to ensure their safety. Both California and Arizona have bypassed this proven approval process, thereby setting a dangerous precedent.

There is a FDA-approved alternative to marijuana.

A synthetic form of delta-9-tetrahydrocannabinol (THC), the main psychoactive ingredient of marijuana, has been approved by the FDA as an anti-nausea agent for cancer chemotherapy patients and as an appetite stimulant for patients with AIDS Wasting Syndrome. Unlike marijuana, synthetic THC ("Marinol") is a stable, well-defined, pure substance in quantified dosage form.

Even though Marinol is FDA-approved, it has many drawbacks. The producers of Marinol say the following: "Because of its profound effects on the mental status, patients should be warned not to drive, operate complex machinery, or engage in any activity requiring sound judgment and unimpaired coordination while receiving Marinol."[18]

Marijuana is a dangerous drug

Allowing marijuana as medicine makes drug abuse more likely.

Drug czar Barry McCaffrey believes that passage of the California and Arizona propositions will result in more abuse. "By our judgment," McCaffrey says, "increased drug abuse in every category will be the inevitable result of the referenda."[19]

Drug abuse has risen dramatically over the past few years. The 1995 National Household Survey on Drug Abuse found that an estimated 12.8 million Americans were current illicit drug abusers. In 1992, the rate of past-month illicit drug abuse by adolescents (ages 12 to 17) reached a low of 5.3 percent. By 1995 it had climbed to 8.2 percent and in August 1996 it is at 10.9 percent. That is a 105 percent increase.[20]

In 1995, the teen drug of choice was marijuana. The rate of past-month use of marijuana jumped 33 percent between 1994 and 1995. Since 1992, the rate has more than doubled.[21]

Marijuana acts as a gateway for other drug use. A 1994 Columbia University study prepared by the Center on Addiction and Substance Abuse found that children who have used marijuana are more than 85 times more likely to use cocaine than children who have never used marijuana.[22]

Marijuana is addictive.

Marijuana is addictive for some people. Pro-drug groups admitted in court that "marijuana has a high potential for abuse and that abuse may lead to severe psychological or physical dependence."[23] This dependence and associated "addictive" behaviors have been well described in the literature. Marijuana dependence consists of both physical dependence (tolerance and subsequent withdrawal) and a psychological dependence.[24]

Chemicals in marijuana are fat-soluble, which means they do not pass through the body, but leave the bloodstream and embed themselves in cell membranes. Withdrawal from marijuana addiction is a long process because the embedded chemicals are released slowly. Each year 100,000 people are treated for marijuana addiction which is characterized by anxiety, depression, sleep and appetite disturbances, shakiness and irritability.[25]

Today, marijuana addiction is more serious than before because creative pot farming techniques have resulted in powerful new strains of marijuana which may be 30 times stronger than the pot used at the famed 1969 Woodstock music concert.[26] Extended use of potent marijuana strains extends the difficult withdrawal period.

Marijuana use is associated with many adverse health effects.

Donna Shalala, Secretary of Health & Human Services, said: "There is clear scientific evidence that marijuana is harmful to one's brain, heart, and lungs. It limits learning, memory, perception, judgment and complex motor skills like those needed to drive a vehicle. It has been shown to damage motivation and interest in one's goals and activities. It can cause chronic coughing and bronchitis. In short, it is a very dangerous drug."[27]

No FDA approved drug is administered by smoking.

A byproduct of smoking crude marijuana for "medicine" is that it increases the patient's chances of lung cancer. "There is good scientific evidence showing adverse effects of smoking marijuana," says Billy Martin, a professor at the Virginia Commonwealth University's medical college. "Certainly it has much higher tar content than cigarettes."[28] One study found that marijuana smoking resulted in up to four times the respiratory burden of an equivalent amount of tobacco smoking.[29] A September, 1993, National Institute on Drug Abuse update reported, "Daily use of one to three marijuana joints appears to produce approximately the same lung damage and potential cancer risk as smoking five times as many cigarettes."[30]

Defining marijuana as medicine sends the wrong message to our children.

"Changes in attitudes drive changes in behavior," said Ginna Marston, director of research and strategic development for Partnership for a Drug-Free America (PDFA). "These findings tell us one thing: drug use will continue increasing among teenagers until these attitudes change."[31]

Labeling marijuana as "medicine" communicates that it is a safe substance. That message will likely further erode the perceived risk in drug use by teen-agers. According to PDFA, the number of teens who agree with the statement "taking drugs scares me" declined from 47 percent in 1993 to 36 percent in 1995.[32]

Allowing marijuana as medicine makes drug abuse more likely.

The courts have declared marijuana a dangerous drug with no medical use.

The National Organization for Reform of Marijuana Laws (NORML), Alliance for Cannabis Therapeutics (ACT) and the Cannabis Corporation of America petitioned the Drug Enforcement Administration to reschedule marijuana from a Schedule I drug (unable to be prescribed, high potential for abuse, not currently accepted for medicinal use, and lack of safety of the drug) to a Schedule II drug (high potential for abuse, currently accepted for medical use, potential for abuse, but able to be prescribed).[33]

Administrative law Judge Francis Young was asked by the Drug Enforcement Administration (DEA) in 1988 to rule on the merits of rescheduling. Young relied heavily on anecdotal information presented from the pro-pot movement. Virtually ignoring the volumes of evidence which opposed the move to reschedule marijuana, the judge ruled that marijuana should be rescheduled to Schedule II for nausea associated with cancer chemotherapy. He concluded, however, that insufficient evidence existed to warrant use of crude marijuana for glaucoma. His decision has become the centerpiece for the pro-marijuana movement.

Despite Judge Young's decision, the DEA administrator denied the petition to reschedule. He turned to numerous nationally recognized experts who had studied the issue extensively. During hearings it became clear that crude pot has not been accepted as a medicine by medical associations.

On February 18, 1994, the U.S. Court of Appeals for the District of Columbia Circuit established guidelines requiring rigorous scientific proof in order to satisfy the requirement of "currently accepted medical use."[34] Crude marijuana does not meet these guidelines.

The Court said of the DEA administrator's decision denying scheduling, "The administrator reasonably accorded more weight to the opinions of the experts than to the laymen and doctors on which the petitioners relied."[35]

The dangerous legalization movement

Calls for medical marijuana laws will reach every state.

Bill Zimmerman, manager of the successful California campaign promised to take his medical marijuana movement on the road. He will name it "Americans for Medical Rights." He promises to pursue a congressional lobbying strategy to win federal legislation and to seek similar initiatives in other states.[36]

Marijuana as medicine has always been a "red herring" for drug legalization.

In 1979, Keith Stroup, NORML's founder, announced that they [NORML] would be using the issue of medical marijuana as a "red herring" to give marijuana a good name.[37]

The drug legalizers have deep pockets.

The California and Arizona propositions were primarily funded by well known drug legalizers. George Soros, a New York City-based billionaire money manager, has given perhaps $15 million to various drug legalization groups since 1991 including a million dollars to support the successful proposition campaigns.[38]

Mr. Soros reportedly gave the pro-drug Drug Policy Foundation six million dollars with a "set of suggestions to follow." These included: "Come up with an approach that emphasizes 'treatment and humanitarian endeavors,'. . . like medical marijuana."[39]

John Sperling, who gave $630,000 to support the initiatives, said, "The drug problem is a public health problem primarily. It only becomes a crime when you put people in prison for it." People who deny this are "either intellectually dishonest, stupid, or both, and that goes for most members of Congress, the President, and the man who wanted to be President."[40]

Consequences of further legalization

More propositions like those in California and Arizona will weaken law enforcement efforts and could eventually lead to outright drug legalization.

The pro-drug referenda will only fuel the calls for legalization in an already drug saturated culture.

Much of the pop culture is pro-marijuana. Select music groups encourage marijuana legalization. In 1995, Capricorn Records released *Hempilation*, a benefit album for NORML. At least 45 bands have declared support for legalizing marijuana.

Marijuana abuse is lightly portrayed or treated as inconsequential behavior. The number of anti-drug-related stories airing on the three major television networks between 1989 and 1994 declined by more than 83 percent.

The marijuana fashion craze in the early 1990s attracted wide media attention. This craze is being supplanted by "heroin chic" popularized by commercial enterprises like Calvin Klein.
More drug use will increase medical costs.
Drug use studies consistently find that as the perception of risk declines, use rises. In 1996, every major drug survey found that adolescents perceived less risk associated with marijuana use than in the prior year. This explains, in part, the skyrocketing rates of use which translates into dramatic increases in health costs.
The national Drug Abuse Warning Network (DAWN) reports a surge in marijuana-related emergency room visits. The 1995 DAWN survey found that marijuana continued to be mentioned more often than any other substance in drug-related hospital emergencies. Between 1994 and 1995, marijuana-related episodes rose 17 percent.[41]

Defining marijuana as medicine sends the wrong message to our children.

Expect more marijuana-impaired drivers.
California decriminalized marijuana in 1976, and, within the first six months, arrests for driving under the influence of drugs rose 46 percent for adults and 71.4 percent for juveniles.[42] Decriminalizing marijuana in Alaska and Oregon in the 1970s resulted in the doubling of use.[43]
Unlike alcohol, an officer has no test available to immediately determine if a driver is under the influence of marijuana. In alcohol related cases, most drivers choose a non-invasive breath test which can be administered in the field. The officer instantly knows if alcohol is a factor in poor driving behavior.
Detecting marijuana-related intoxication is more difficult. It requires an invasive blood or urine-based test and often takes days to complete. If a driver claims he has medically legal marijuana, the case could become extremely difficult or impossible to prosecute.
Marijuana abuse among drivers has long been a problem. A 1993 study assessed the impact of alcohol and other drug use in the trucking industry. Drug screens performed on blood specimens collected from 168 fatally injured drivers found 67 percent of the drivers had recently used one or more drugs. The most prevalent drugs were cannabinoids [marijuana] and ethanol, each found in 13 percent of the drivers.[44]
A study published in the *New England Journal of Medicine* in 1993 tested a consecutive-sample of subjects arrested for reckless driving who were not apparently impaired by alcohol. Fifty-nine percent tested positive for illicit drugs. Fully a third of these had used marijuana.[45]
A 1996 study of marijuana users found that heavy users displayed significantly greater impairment than light users on attentional functions. The study concludes that heavy marijuana use results in residual neuropsychological effects even after a day of supervised abstinence from the drug.[46]
The propositions create other law enforcement problems.
Senator Orrin Hatch, chairman, U.S. Senate Judiciary Committee, il-

lustrated one legal consequence of the new laws. "Suppose a California law enforcement officer discovers someone in possession of marijuana who claims to have obtained marijuana based on the oral 'communication' of a local physician for relief of 'nausea.' An officer confronting that situation faces a conundrum. He may not be able to make an arrest because he may not have probable cause to believe that a crime has occurred under state law."[47]

A prisoner who acquires a doctor's oral or written approval to use marijuana [now only in California and Arizona] might be within his rights to use the substance and the state might be obligated to provide the drug.

Are police officers liable if they let individuals with marijuana, who claim a medical condition, drive off and later injure or kill someone?

How should law enforcement officers respond to large marijuana gardens when the owners claim that they are "caregivers" who must cultivate marijuana for their "patients?"

There are implications for businesses.

There will be conflicts between the federal contractual necessity of providing a drug free workplace with the claims of employees that they have a medical requirement to use prescribed Schedule I drugs.

There are foreign policy concerns.

The U.S. has treaty obligations to eradicate the production and dissemination of drugs. Medical use laws confuse the situation. Similar laws in The Netherlands have seriously strained their relations with neighboring European countries.

Other issues

Marijuana use is linked to homicide.

A 1994 New York State study found that marijuana abuse was a common thread in 268 murderers. About one-third of the murderers had used pot in the 24-hour period before the homicide, and three-quarters of those said they experienced some kind of effect from the drug when the homicide occurred.[48]

"Marijuana-as-medicine" marginalizes the U.S. Government's sincere efforts to study pot for its adverse and possible beneficial attributes.

Since the 1970s more than 12,000 scientific studies have been conducted on marijuana. The marijuana (cannabis) used in the studies is obtained from the Research Institute of Pharmaceutical Sciences at the University of Mississippi, which produces a standardized marijuana specifically for research. Material to be used in clinical trials is shipped to Research Triangle Institute in North Carolina where it is processed into marijuana cigarettes. It is then made available for Researchers following proper protocol approved by the National Institute on Drug Abuse.[49]

The U.S. Government has given marijuana to a select few "for medical reasons."

Twenty years ago the University of Mississippi began supplying a select group of patients with marijuana under a separate program, overseen by the FDA, to provide "compassionate care" to relieve symptoms from diseases like multiple sclerosis, epilepsy, cancer, glaucoma and rare genetic diseases. Under the Compassionate Investigative New Drug program (IND) eight patients are supplied with up to 300 marijuana cigarettes a month. This program stopped taking new patients in 1992.[50]

The project is not a research study intended to evaluate the medicinal value of marijuana, however. Don McLearn, a spokesman for the FDA, says, "It is not a clinical trial. There was never any intent of using reports from the compassionate IND's to reach approval for the drug."[51]

In 1994, the Department of Health and Human Services reconsidered whether the single patient IND process would be helpful in providing scientific evidence to support the various claims of benefits. After consultation with experts in the design of clinical studies, it is clear that the single patient IND process is not the type of clinical trial that would produce useful scientific information and would not be adequate for demonstrating safety and efficacy for the FDA approval process.[52]

What should people do?

Oppose legislation and/or propositions that seek to legalize marijuana as medicine.

Expect well-funded, pro-drug groups to introduce medical marijuana propositions and/or legislation. Take the threat seriously by organizing to educate the citizens and leaders.

Rescind statutes that endorse medical use of marijuana.

Paul Armentano of NORML, says, at one time, 34 states had passed "some endorsement of a medical use of marijuana." Twenty-three states in 1997 have laws allowing the medical use of marijuana. Today, Armentano says, "those laws are largely symbolic, because they are at odds with federal law, and federal law supersedes state law."[53] So-called "symbolic" laws ought to be rescinded before they find new life.

To the surprise of Virginia State Delegate Bob Marshall, the Commonwealth of Virginia has a statute that allows medical doctors to prescribe marijuana. No doubt other legislators in Virginia and elsewhere will be surprised to discover that their states also have laws which permit the "medical" use of crude marijuana.

Educate citizens about marijuana.

Marijuana is a misunderstood and dangerous drug. Use private and public means to spread the word. . . .

How should law enforcement officers respond to large marijuana gardens when the owners claim that they are "caregivers" who must cultivate marijuana for their "patients"?

Learn from previously failed legalization efforts.

Pot was decriminalized in Alaska between 1975 and 1991. Possession of up to four ounces by an adult was lawful but the purchase, sale and distribution of marijuana continued to be illegal. Marijuana use among Alaskan teenagers doubled. In 1990, an anti-drug referendum struck down "legal" marijuana.

Keep marijuana a Schedule I drug.

The federal Controlled Substances Act of 1970 schedules drugs according to their effects, medical use and potential abuse. Schedule I drugs are those defined as having "a high potential for abuse . . . no currently accepted medical use in treatment in the United States. . . [and] a lack of accepted safety for use of the drug or other substance under medical supervision." Schedule I drugs include marijuana, heroin, LSD, hashish, methaqualone and designer drugs.

"Medical" approval for illicit Schedule I drugs creates special problems for society.

Parents must be the first line of defense.

Ultimately, America's adolescent drug abuse problem will only be minimized if parents, teachers, coaches, ministers and counselors running youth-oriented organizations motivate young Americans to reject drugs. Keeping kids drug free is critical because as Columbia University's CASA reports, children who escape their teen years without using illicit drugs will likely never become abusers. Stopping adolescent abuse will dramatically reduce the scope of the future illicit drug use and addiction problem.

Do not extradite illegal drug abusers back to California and Arizona but prosecute them using local, state or federal laws.

California and Arizona law enforcement officials have already found drug users reaching beyond state lines. On December 2, 1996, Los Angeles County Sheriff Brad Gates told the U.S. Senate Judiciary Committee that a California "care provider" tried to mail ten pounds of marijuana to his "sick" brother in Ohio. This scenario complicates for the other 48 states compliance with the Constitution's Full Faith and Credit provision (Article IV, sections 1 & 2). This Constitutional provision means that states recognize one another's laws. In the case of state-approved "medical" use of Schedule I drugs, each state must decide how to treat visitors from California and Arizona who are "care providers" and those with "legal" Schedule I prescriptions.

All political, cultural and civic leaders must use consistent and strong anti-drug messages.

A winning strategy requires leaders with vision and the authority to enforce their policies. Recent presidents have given too much responsibility to the drug czar who has virtually no authority. The President must give this issue considerable personal attention.

The president can't do this alone, though. All leaders must become responsible role models and actively participate in promoting healthy drug messages.

Develop policies with regard to non-FDA approved drugs.

Illicit drug entrepreneurs will continue to seek out new drugs e.g., crack, Rohypnol and designer drugs. Government must be prepared to quickly adopt policies to safeguard citizens from dangerous fad-like drugs.

Ascertain and publicize government's responsibilities and liabilities when Schedule I drugs like marijuana are approved for "medical" use.

Use of Schedule I drugs is strictly controlled. When states stiff-arm federal law to approve "medical" use of Schedule I drugs they inherit responsibilities and liabilities which should be publicized. Citizens have a right to know the costs associated with "medical" use of otherwise illicit substances.

Develop state and local comprehensive and long-term emergency drug prevention plans.

After great strides to curb the drug scourge in the 1980s, America took its eye off drug use and now the problem is getting worse. Rising abuse is being fueled by the "medical marijuana" movement. To reverse this trend, government must develop a comprehensive and long-term community-based drug prevention plan. The plan should include: zero tolerance for drug legalization; drug education resources tied to accountability measures; drug education messages consistently broadcast through every educational setting; identification of drug users and consequences to reduce demand; accountability for drug abuse prevention at the local level; and grassroots/citizen action groups with power over funds to make local programs work.

Alert and educate businesses, law enforcement, schools and citizens about the ramifications of "medical use" of Schedule I drugs.

"Medical" approval for illicit Schedule I drugs creates special problems for society. Businesses need to understand whether they can remove Schedule I drug users from certain jobs. Law enforcement needs clarification when dealing with the presence of "medically" approved Schedule I drugs at traffic violation scenes, for prison inmates, and in situations which include chance discoveries.

Taking a stand

The California and Arizona propositions send the message that drug use is okay thus confusing good medicine with quackery and abuse. Drug legalizers have wrapped their radical desires in "compassion" while aiming for free access to all now-illicit Schedule I drugs. Expect these radicals to march across this nation employing all the weapons in their arsenal to expand their two-state foothold. Time is short and leaders must take decisive action to stand against this insidious movement.

Notes

1. Statement by General Barry R. McCaffrey, Director, Office of National Drug Control Policy, to the U.S. Senate Committee on the Judiciary, 2 December 1996.

2. Statement of Senator Orrin G. Hatch, Senate Committee on the Judiciary, Hearing on Medical Uses of Marijuana, 2 December 1996.

3. *Ibid.*

4. "Medicinal Marijuana Briefing Paper." A publication of the Marijuana Policy Project, P.O. Box 77492, Capitol Hill, Washington, DC 20013, Autumn 1995.

5. Donna J. Schroeder, et al. "DIAS Rounds." *The Annals of Pharmacotherapy.* Vol. 28, May 1994:595.

6. "National Institute on Allergy and Infectious Diseases Factsheet on the Therapeutic Use of Marijuana for Patients with HIV-Wasting Syndrome." National Institutes of Health, Department of Health & Human Services, Public Health Service, Bethesda, Maryland attached to a letter from Philip R. Lee, Assistant Secretary for Health, Department of Health & Human

Services for Rep. Dan Hamburg, House of Representatives, Washington, DC, 13 July 1994.

7. "Medicinal Marijuana Briefing Paper," *Op cit.*

8. "National Eye Institute Fact Sheet on the Therapeutic Use of Marijuana for Glaucoma." National Institutes of Health, Department of Health & Human Services, Public Health Service, Bethesda, Maryland, not dated. This fact sheet was attached to a letter from Philip R. Lee, Assistant Secretary of Health for Rep. Dan Hamburg, House of Representatives, Washington, DC, 13 July 1994.

9. Cited in testimony of John P. Walters, former Acting Director and Deputy Director for Supply Reduction of the Office of National Drug Control Policy, before the Committee on the Judiciary of the United States Senate, 2 December 1996.

10. Cited in the testimony of John P. Walters, former Acting Director and Deputy Director for Supply Reduction of the Office of National Drug Control Policy, before the Committee on the Judiciary of the United States Senate, 2 December 1996.

11. "Medicinal Marijuana Briefing Paper," *Op cit.*

12. Letter from Harmon J. Eyre, MD, Executive Vice President for Research & Cancer Control, American Cancer Society, 1599 Clifton Road, NE, Atlanta, GA for Stephanie Haynes, President, Drug Watch International, PO Box 1022, Alpine, TX, 2 July 1996.

13. Joyce Price. "Marijuana Initiative Poses Legal Quandary." *The Washington Times*. 1 December 1996:A-1.

14. Cited in John Walters, *Op cit.*

15. "Medical Marijuana Briefing Paper," *Op cit.*

16. Harry S. Greenberg. "Short-term effects of smoking marijuana on balance in patients with multiple sclerosis and normal volunteers." *Clinical Pharmacology & Therapeutics*, Vol. 55, No. 3, 1994:324.

17. "National Institute of Neurological Disorders and Stroke Factsheet on the Therapeutic Use of Marijuana for Multiple Sclerosis." National Institutes of Health, Department of Health & Human Services, Bethesda, Maryland, undated. This factsheet was attached to a letter from Philip R. Lee, assistant Secretary for Health to Rep. Dan Hamburg, House of Representatives, Washington, DC, 13 July 1994.

18. Marinol. *Physicians' Desk Reference.* 1993:46:1985–1987.

19. Statement by General McCaffrey, *Op cit.*

20. "Preliminary Estimates from the 1995 National Household Survey on Drug Abuse." U.S. Department of Health & Human Services, Public Health Service, Substance Abuse and Mental Health Services Administration, Office of Applied Studies, Advance Report No. 18, August 1996.

21. *Ibid.*

22. Cited in statement by Barry McCaffrey, *Op cit.*

23. Francis Young. Opinion and recommended ruling, marijuana rescheduling petition. United States Department of Justice, Drug Enforcement Administration, Docket 86-22. September 1988.

24. Eric A. Voth. "Marijuana: Alleged Medicinal Uses—Physical and Social Consequences." The International Drug Strategy Institute, 901 Garfield, Topeka, Kansas, 20 October 1995.

25. "Marijuana: Facts Parents Need to Know." National Institute of Drug Abuse, National Institutes of Health. 1995:22-23.

26. Eric A. Voth, *Op cit.*

27. Statement by General McCaffrey, *Op cit.*

28. Daniel P. Ray. "Marijuana Use Linked to Cancer." *The Miami Herald.* 8 February 1994.

29. Tzu-Chin Wu, et al. "Pulmonary Hazards of Smoking Marijuana as Compared with Tobacco." *New England Journal of Medicine.* Vol. 318. 1988:347-351.

30. "Marijuana Update." National Institute on Drug Abuse, *Capsules* newsletter. September, 1994:2.

31. "Adolescent Drug Use Likely to Increase Again in '96; Teens See Fewer Risks in Marijuana and Drug Use." Partnership for a Drug-Free America, New York, NY, 20 February 1996.

32. *Ibid.*

33. Cited in Eric Voth, *Op cit.*

34. *Ibid.*

35. *Ibid.*

36. Catherine Moser. "Medical Marijuana." *Voice of America*, correspondent report #2.205777, 6 November 1996.

37. *Emory Wheel.* February, 1979.

38. Carey Goldberg, *Op cit.*

39. Cited in John Walters, *Op cit.*

40. *Ibid.*

41. "National Drug Survey Results Released," *Op cit.*

42. Peggy Mann, "Reasons to Oppose Legalizing Illegal Drugs." Published by Committee of Correspondence, Inc., Danvers, MA, September 1988.

43. Wayne J. Roques. "Decriminalizing Drugs Would Be a Disaster." *The Miami Herald*, 20 January 1995.

44. Dennis J. Crouch, et al. "The Prevalence of Drugs and Alcohol in Fatally Injured Truck Drivers." *Journal of Forensic Sciences*, Vol. 38, No. 6, November 1993:1342.

45. Daniel Brookoff et al. "Testing Reckless Drivers for Cocaine and Marijuana." *The New England Journal of Medicine*, Vol. 331, 25 August 1994:518.

46. Harrison G. Ope and Deborah Yurgelun-Todd. "The Residual Cognitive Effects of Heavy Marijuana Use in College Students." *The Journal of the American Medical Association*, Vol. 275, No. 7, 21 February 1996:521.

47. Statement of Senator Hatch, *Op cit.*

48. Marijuana Research Review, Vol. 2, No. 1, January 1995.

49. Marijuana Research Review, Vol. 1, No. 2, July 1994.

50. "Despite Marijuana Furor, 8 Users Get It From the Government." *The New York Times*. 1 December 1996:33.

51. *Ibid.*

52. Philip R. Lee, *Op cit.*

53. Joyce Price. "States wrangle over medical pot laws." *The Washington Times*. 1 December 1996:A-7.

12

Marijuana Is Not Safe or Effective Medicine

Paul Leithart

Paul Leithart is a doctor with more than twenty years of experience in treating substance abuse.

Marijuana's claimed healing powers with regards to glaucoma, cancer, and pain relief have not been proven by scientific studies. Because of its damaging effects to the brain and lungs, marijuana should be considered a health hazard rather than medicine. The media should fully inform the public about the dangers of smoking marijuana.

For centuries *Cannabis sativa* has been known as a mind-altering hallucinogen. In the 1960s it became the *sine qua non* of the counterculture (the era of the pothead). In the 1990s it has evolved into "medical marijuana," the miracle drug capable of relieving virtually all pain and disease.

What is the truth about marijuana? Does it have medicinal value? How did it become transformed from an illicit, outlawed weed to serious consideration as a vital medicine?

Problems with marijuana

There has been more extensive research on marijuana over the past 40 years than on any other substance. Marijuana contains over 420 compounds, including 60 cannabinoids (the psychoactive ingredients). Delta 9 THC, a tetra-hydro-cannabinol, is the most active in producing the high people seek from marijuana.

Cannabinoids from a single marijuana cigarette deposit in the fatty tissue of the body (brain, testes, ovaries, etc.) and remain there for three to four weeks. Repeated use of the drug produces THC storage in these vital organs for months. By contrast, when alcohol is consumed it is metabolized in a few hours.

Contrary to the arguments of its advocates, marijuana is physically and psychologically addictive. Additionally, when a user stops he experi-

Reprinted from Paul Leithart, "Marijuana as Medicine," *The New American*, October 13, 1997, by permission of *The New American*.

ences withdrawal symptoms. Also, myriads of psychological symptoms develop as use becomes chronic.

When a joint is inhaled, over 2,000 noxious chemicals invade the lungs.

When a joint is inhaled, over 2,000 noxious chemicals invade the lungs. Users typically "toke," holding the smoke in their lungs to enhance the absorption of THC. This produces more rapid lung damage than smoking tobacco. Marijuana and tobacco share the same chemical compounds (except for the cannabinoids), but somehow cigarettes are deemed the more deadly, while pot is touted as a medical necessity.

The high from pot has been described by its users as a euphoria, a pleasant, relaxed escape that causes one to become self-absorbed and to pay less attention to his surroundings. The anticipation of these sensations is the major reason for use. And with repeated use, one's ability to think becomes dulled, concentration is more difficult, and pathological thinking develops. The ability to perform tasks—especially new ones—diminishes, the memory becomes impaired, the sense of time is altered, and an inertia or lack of motivation develops. In many users an amotivational syndrome sets in.

Chronic users often develop such problems as emotional instability, difficulty in absorbing and integrating new information, and decreased work performance. As the brain's "pleasure center" becomes exhausted, users have difficulty in experiencing pleasure and often put forth less effort to socialize. Users go from a sense of suspiciousness to a full-blown paranoia—and, eventually, to total "burnout."

Marijuana's effectiveness

In spite of the documented side effects associated with marijuana use, it has nonetheless been promoted as useful in the treatment of an amazing variety of ailments. Unfortunately, the truth about marijuana's effectiveness in treating physical maladies is completely overblown:

• *Glaucoma.* Proponents claim pot smoking lowers the pressure in the eyes of glaucoma patients. A small pressure drop does occur in some patients when marijuana is used every two to four hours around the clock. This would mean, of course, that the user would be constantly stoned. In many users the pressure increases, however, and recent research indicates that pot users have a decreased circulation to the optic nerve—a serious problem. Also, there have been medications available for years that are as effective as marijuana and that have minimal side effects.

• *Cancer.* Marijuana is advocated to fight nausea in patients receiving intensive chemotherapy. But it is really no better than the many safer antinauseants available. Also, pot has been found to damage the immune system, which is important in fighting cancer and other serious ailments like AIDS, infection, etc.

• *Pain.* Pot is not an analgesic. For example, users frequently have toothaches which are not relieved with their pot smoking; they require the standard pain killers. Marijuana is not helpful in fighting other kinds of pain either.

In short, all the "medical uses" for marijuana, including asthma, seizures, multiple sclerosis, muscle spasms, etc., are really just excuses to get high. Some users may be under the delusion they are being helped, but pot users typically smoke for the THC while still taking the standard medications for their disease. Synthetic Delta 9THC (Marinol) is available by prescription for some conditions and is effective. Pot users say they prefer the side effects from pot to the side effects of prescription drugs, however.

NORML's "red herring"

In essence, then, rather than being a medicine, marijuana is a health hazard. Who would call a drug "recreational" if they realized that chronic use causes permanent brain damage? Pot use is never cited by proponents as a factor in high school dropout and failure rates, as well as the increase in promiscuity and sexually transmitted diseases. Such is the case, however. Another area they ignore is the dramatic effect pot has on the ability for one to drive a car safely. Not only is the driver impaired in major ways while high, but for hours after the high wears off. Why are these important facts not better understood by the public?

For more than 35 years the media have suppressed information on pot. The National Institute on Drug Abuse (NIDA) published an annual report on "Marijuana and Health" for many years—each issue cataloging the increasing THC content of the weed and the dramatic research findings on damage to the user's body. These reports have been ignored by the media, although all levels of media outlets were supplied with NIDA findings.

Prescribing pot for any medical condition is totally irresponsible.

In 1971 the National Organization for the Reform of Marijuana Laws (NORML) was founded. It soon became a highly organized and influential body. There are 80,000 members, with attorney members in many larger cities. NORML conducts seminars to train lawyers in defending users and pushers when they are arrested. The hearings in state houses across the country are highly choreographed by these lawyers. They often call in NORML's national advisers—Lester Grinspoon, MD and Thomas Ungerleider, MD—for the hearings. For many years these two psychiatrists have been major activists in the pot war. Dr. Grinspoon declares that marijuana is a "wonderful medicine" and finds it useful for almost every malady. Users who have major medical problems are featured witnesses at hearings. These patients declare that they would be dead except for their pot. The media (especially television) feature these experts and patients, usually ignoring the testimony of legitimate medical experts.

If marijuana is legalized there are billions of dollars to be made by the unscrupulous. Billionaire financier George Soros, who admits to having experimented with pot, gave a million dollars for the California and Arizona pro-pot initiatives.

The Federal Drug Administration issues narcotic licenses to physicians. Under license guidelines, Schedule 1 substances "have no accepted medical use . . . and have a high abuse potential." Included in this category are heroin, marijuana, and LSD. Any physician, however, can receive marijuana for use in legitimate medical research. But pot users want free access to the drug. Furthermore, the Psychotropic Convention Treaty of 1971 classifies marijuana as a Schedule 1 drug. The U.S. is one of the 74 nations that have accepted the treaty.

In 1974 the director of NORML, Keith Stroup, was interviewed for a student paper at Emory University. He was asked about using marijuana with chemotherapy patients and answered, "We are trying to get marijuana reclassified medically . . . we'll be using the issue as a red herring to give marijuana a good name."

A fascinating article, "The Return of Pot," by Hanna Rubin, appeared in the February 17, 1997 issue of *The New Republic*. A visit by Rubin to San Francisco's Cannabis Cultivators Club demonstrated the total absurdity of state-sanctioned use of pot. Rubin stated, "It is as if the rotting of the late '60s San Francisco described by Joan Didion in *Slouching Toward Bethlehem* has been preserved in reverse; the characters are the same, but the center was holding." Rubin recounted the lives of the burnt out beings who frequent these clubs and made it obvious that "medical marijuana" is the red herring that NORML plotted. The article should be must reading for state legislators facing the issue of legalizing "medical marijuana."

The bottom line

Using marijuana for illness would be like a physician prescribing moldy bread (containing penicillin) for pneumonia or suggesting cigarette smoking for stress or weight loss. Prescribing pot for any medical condition is totally irresponsible. Some doctors do and are either naïve about the damage marijuana causes or perhaps are users themselves.

Organizations to Contact

The editors have compiled the following list of organizations concerned with the issues debated in this book. The descriptions are derived from materials provided by the organizations. All have publications or information available for interested readers. The list was compiled on the date of publication of the present volume; the information provided here may change. Be aware that many organizations take several weeks or longer to respond to inquiries, so allow as much time as possible.

American Civil Liberties Union (ACLU)
125 Broad St., 18th Fl., New York, NY 10004-2400
(212) 549-2500
e-mail: aclu@aclu.org • website: http://www.aclu.org

The ACLU is a national organization that works to defend Americans' civil rights guaranteed by the U.S. Constitution. It provides legal defense, research, and education. The ACLU opposes the criminal prohibition of marijuana and the civil liberties violations that result from it. Its publications include *ACLU Briefing Paper #19: Against Drug Prohibition* and *Ira Glasser on Marijuana Myths and Facts*.

American Council for Drug Education (ACDE)
164 W. 74th St., New York, NY 10023
(800) 488-DRUG (3784) • (212) 595-5810, ext. 7860 • fax: (212) 595-2553
website: http://www.acde.org

The American Council for Drug Education informs the public about the harmful effects of abusing drugs and alcohol. It gives the public access to scientifically based, compelling prevention programs and materials. ACDE has resources for parents, youth, educators, prevention professionals, employers, health care professionals, and other concerned community members who are working to help America's youth avoid the dangers of drug and alcohol abuse.

Canadian Foundation for Drug Policy (CFDP)
70 MacDonald St., Ottawa, ON K2P 1H6 CANADA
(613) 236-1027 • fax: (613) 238-2891
e-mail: eoscapel@fox.nstn.ca
website: http://fox.nstn.ca/~eoscapel/cfdp/cfdp.html

Founded by several of Canada's leading drug policy specialists, CFDP examines the objectives and consequences of Canada's drug laws and policies, including laws prohibiting marijuana. When necessary, the foundation recommends alternatives that it believes would make Canada's drug policies more effective and humane. CFDP discusses drug policy issues with the Canadian government, media, and general public. It also disseminates educational materials and maintains a website.

86   *At Issue*

Drug Enforcement Administration (DEA)
700 Army Navy Dr., Arlington, VA 22202
(202) 307-1000
website: http://www.usdoj.gov/deahome.htm

The DEA is the federal agency charged with enforcing the nation's drug laws. The agency concentrates on stopping the smuggling and distribution of narcotics in the United States and abroad. It publishes the *Drug Enforcement Magazine* three times a year.

Drug Policy Foundation
4455 Connecticut Ave. NW, Suite B-500, Washington, DC 20008-2328
(202) 537-5005 • fax: (202) 537-3007
e-mail: dpf@dpf.org • website: http://www.dpf.org

The foundation, an independent nonprofit organization, supports and publicizes alternatives to current U.S. policies on illegal drugs, including marijuana. The foundation's publications include the bimonthly *Drug Policy Letter* and the book *The Great Drug War*. It also distributes *Press Clips*, an annual compilation of newspaper articles on drug legalization issues, as well as legislative updates.

Family Research Council
801 G St. NW, Washington, DC 20001
(202) 393-2100 • order line: (800) 225-4008 • fax: (202) 393-2134
e-mail: corrdept@frc.org • website: http://www.frc.org

The council analyzes issues affecting the family and seeks to ensure that the interests of the traditional family are considered in the formulation of public policy. It lobbies legislatures and promotes public debate on issues concerning the family. The council publishes articles and position papers against the legalization of medicinal marijuana.

Lindesmith Center
400 W. 59th St., New York, NY 10019
(212) 548-0695 • fax: (212) 548-4670
e-mail: lindesmith@sorosny.org • website: http://www.lindesmith.org

The Lindesmith Center is a policy research institute that focuses on broadening the debate on drug policy and related issues. The center houses a library and information center; organizes seminars and conferences; acts as a link between scholars, government, and the media; directs a grant program in Europe; and undertakes projects on drug policy topics, including medicinal marijuana. It addresses issues of drug policy reform through a variety of projects, including the Drug Policy Seminar series, the International Harm Reduction Development Program, and the Methadone Policy Reform Project. The center's website includes articles, polls, and legal documents relating to marijuana.

Marijuana Policy Project
PO Box 77492-Capitol Hill, Washington, DC 20013
(202) 462-5747 • fax: (202) 232-0442
e-mail: mpp@mpp.org • website: http://www.mpp.org

The Marijuana Policy Project develops and promotes policies to minimize the harm associated with marijuana. It is the only organization that is solely concerned with lobbying to reform the marijuana laws on the federal level. The project increases public awareness through speaking engagements, educational seminars, the mass media, and briefing papers.

Multidisciplinary Association for Psychedelic Studies (MAPS)
2121 Commonwealth Ave., Suite 220, Charlotte, NC 28205
(704) 334-1798 • fax: (704) 334-1799
e-mail: info@maps.org • website: http://www.maps.org

MAPS is a membership-based research and educational organization. It focuses on the development of beneficial, socially sanctioned uses of psychedelic drugs and marijuana. MAPS helps scientific researchers obtain governmental approval for, fund, conduct, and report on psychedelic research in human volunteers. It publishes the quarterly *MAPS Bulletin* as well as various reports and newsletters.

National Center on Addiction and Substance Abuse (CASA)
Columbia University
152 W. 57th St., New York, NY 10019-3310
(212) 841-5200 • fax: (212) 956-8020
website: http://www.casacolumbia.org

CASA is a private nonprofit organization that works to educate the public about the hazards of chemical dependency. The organization supports treatment as the best way to reduce chemical dependency. It produces publications describing the harmful effects of alcohol and drug addiction and effective ways to address the problem of substance abuse.

National Clearinghouse for Alcohol and Drug Information
PO Box 2345, Rockville, MD 20847-2345
(800) 729-6686 • (301) 468-2600 • fax: (301) 468-6433
e-mail: shs@health.org • website: http://www.health.org

The clearinghouse distributes publications of the U.S. Department of Health and Human Services, the National Institute on Drug Abuse, and other federal agencies concerned with alcohol and drug abuse. Brochure titles include *Tips for Teens About Marijuana*.

National Institute on Drug Abuse (NIDA)
U.S. Department of Health and Human Services
5600 Fishers Ln., Rockville, MD 20857
(301) 443-6245
e-mail: Information@lists.nida.nih.gov
website: http://www.nida.nih.gov

NIDA supports and conducts research on drug abuse—including the yearly Monitoring the Future Survey—to improve addiction prevention, treatment, and policy efforts. It publishes the bimonthly *NIDA Notes* newsletter, the periodic *NIDA Capsules* fact sheets, and a catalog of research reports and public education materials, such as *Marijuana: Facts for Teens* and *Marijuana: Facts Parents Need to Know*.

National Organization for the Reform of Marijuana Laws (NORML)
1001 Connecticut Ave. NW, Suite 710, Washington, DC 20036
(202) 483-5500 • fax: (202) 483-0057
e-mail: natlnorml@aol.com • website: http://www.norml.org

NORML fights to legalize marijuana and to help those who have been convicted and sentenced for possessing or selling marijuana. In addition to pamphlets and position papers, it publishes the newsletter *Marijuana Highpoints*, the bimonthly *Legislative Bulletin* and *Freedom@NORML*, and the monthly *Potpourri*.

NORML Canada
14846 Jane St., King City, ON L7B 1A3 CANADA
(905) 833-3167 • fax: (905) 833-3682
e-mail: iorfida@interlog.com • website: http://www.calyx.com/~normlca/

NORML Canada believes the discouragement of marijuana through use of criminal law has been excessively costly and harmful to both society and individuals. Although it does not advocate or encourage the use of marijuana, NORML Canada works at all levels of government to eliminate criminal penalties for private marijuana use.

Office of National Drug Control Policy
Executive Office of the President
Drugs and Crime Clearinghouse
PO Box 6000, Rockville, MD 20849-6000
e-mail: ondcp@ncjrs.org • website: http://www.whitehousedrugpolicy.gov

The Office of National Drug Control Policy is responsible for formulating the government's national drug strategy and the president's antidrug policy as well as coordinating the federal agencies responsible for stopping drug trafficking. Drug policy studies are available upon request.

Partnership for a Drug-Free America
405 Lexington Ave., Suite 1601, New York, NY 10174
(212) 922-1560 • fax: (212) 922-1570
website: http://www.drugfreeamerica.org

The Partnership for a Drug-Free America is a nonprofit organization that utilizes media communication to reduce demand for illicit drugs in America. Best known for its national antidrug advertising campaign, the partnership works to "unsell" drugs to children and to prevent drug use among kids. It publishes the annual *Partnership Newsletter* as well as monthly press releases about current events with which the partnership is involved.

Bibliography

Books

Dan Baum — *Smoke and Mirrors: The War on Drugs and the Politics of Failure*. Boston: Little, Brown, 1996.

William J. Bennett, John J. DiIulio Jr., and John P. Walters — *Body Count: Moral Poverty—and How to Win America's War on Crime and Drugs*. New York: Simon & Schuster, 1996.

Chris Conrad — *Hemp for Health: The Nutritional and Medicinal Uses of the World's Most Extraordinary Plant*. Rochester, VT: Inner Traditions, 1997.

David R. Ford — *Marijuana: Not Guilty as Charged*. Sonoma, CA: Good Press, 1997.

Lester Grinspoon — *Marijuana Reconsidered: The Most Thorough Evaluation of the Benefits and Dangers of Cannabis*. Cambridge, MA: Harvard University Press, 1996.

Lester Grinspoon and James B. Bakalar — *Marihuana: The Forbidden Medicine*. New Haven, CT: Yale University Press, 1997.

Evan C. Keliher — *Grandpa's Marijuana Handbook*. San Diego: Pedagogue Press, 1997.

Mary Lynn Mathre, ed. — *Cannabis in Medical Practice: A Legal, Historical, and Pharmacological Overview of the Therapeutic Use of Marijuana*. Jefferson, NC: McFarland, 1997.

Richard Lawrence Miller — *Drug Warriors and Their Prey: From Police Power to Police State*. Westport, CT: Praeger, 1996.

Office of National Drug Control Policy — *The National Drug Control Strategy, 1997*. Washington, DC: Executive Office of the President, 1997.

Beverly Potter and Dan Joy — *The Healing Magic of Cannabis*. Berkeley, CA: Ronin, 1998.

Ed Rosenthal, Dale Gieringer, and Tod Mikuriya — *Marijuana Medical Handbook: A Guide to Therapeutic Use*. Oakland, CA: Quick American Archives, 1997.

Ed Rosenthal and Steve Kubby — *Why Marijuana Should Be Legal*. New York: Thunder's Mouth Press, 1996.

Elizabeth Schleichert — *Marijuana*. Springfield, NJ: Enslow, 1996.

Lynn Zimmer and John P. Morgan — *Marijuana Myths; Marijuana Facts: A Review of the Scientific Evidence*. New York: Lindesmith Center, 1997.

Periodicals

George J. Annas	"Reefer Madness—the Federal Response to California's Medical-Marijuana Law," *New England Journal of Medicine,* August 7, 1997. Available from 1440 Main St., Waltham, MA 02154-0413.
Paul Armentano	"The Fight for Medical Marijuana," *Liberty,* January 1998. Available from 1018 Water St., Suite 201, Port Townsend, WA 98368.
Doug Bandow	"Medicine for the Sick," *Freeman,* October 1997. Available from Irvington-on-Hudson, New York, NY 10533.
Dan Baum	"California's Separate Peace," *Rolling Stone,* October 30, 1997.
Dan Baum	"Rx Marijuana," *Nation,* December 2, 1996.
William J. Bennett and John P. Walters	"Medical Reefer Madness," *Weekly Standard,* December 9, 1996. Available from PO Box 96153, Washington, DC 20090-6153.
Robert I. Block	"Does Heavy Marijuana Use Impair Human Cognition and Brain Function?" *JAMA,* February 21, 1996. Available from PO Box 10623, Chicago, IL 60610-0623.
Bruce Bower	"Marijuana's Effects Tracked in Rat Brains," *Science News,* June 28, 1997.
William F. Buckley	"Judicial High in California," *National Review,* February 9, 1998.
Joseph A. Califano Jr.	"Medical Marijuana and the Lesson of Laetrile," *Washington Post National Weekly Edition,* February 24, 1997. Available from 1150 15th St. NW, Washington, DC 20071.
Thomas W. Clark	"Keep Marijuana Illegal—for Teens," *Humanist,* May/June 1997.
Marcus Conant	"This Is Smart Medicine," *Newsweek,* February 3, 1997.
Consumer Reports	"Marijuana as Medicine: How Strong Is the Science?" May 1997.
Steve Diamond	"Taking the High Road," *New Age Journal,* March/April 1996. Available from PO Box 488, Mount Morris, IL 61054-0488.
Sarah Ferguson	"The Battle for Medical Marijuana," *Nation,* January 6, 1997.
Nick Gillespie	"Prescription Drugs," *Reason,* February 1997.
Lester Grinspoon and James B. Bakalar	"Marihuana as Medicine: A Plea for Reconsideration," *JAMA,* June 21, 1995.
Joshua Hammer	"The War over Weed," *Newsweek,* March 16, 1998.
Hendrik Hertzberg	"The Pot Perplex," *New Yorker,* January 6, 1997.

Jerome P. Kassirer — "Federal Foolishness and Marijuana," *New England Journal of Medicine*, January 30, 1997.

Peter McWilliams — "The DEA Wishes Me a Nice Day," *Liberty*, May 1998.

Judy Monroe — "Marijuana—a Mind Altering Drug," *Current Health*, March 1998.

Michael Pollan — "Living with Medical Marijuana," *New York Times Magazine*, July 20, 1997.

Virginia I. Postrel — "Reefer Madness," *Reason*, March 1997.

Brian Preston — "Vancouver's Pot Experiment," *Rolling Stone*, April 2, 1998.

Sarah Richardson — "Better Not Inhale," *Discover*, January 1998.

Hanna Rosin — "The Return of Pot," *New Republic*, February 17, 1997.

Eric Schlosser — "Reefer Madness," *Atlantic Monthly*, August 1994.

Joshua Wolf Shenk — "Just Saying 'No' to the Sick and Suffering," *Washington Monthly*, October 1995.

Cindy Shute — "Reefer Madness," *American Health*, January/February 1996.

Adam J. Smith — "Pot of Trouble," *Reason*, May 1997.

William E. Stempsey — "The Battle for Medical Marijuana in the War on Drugs," *America*, April 11, 1998.

Betsy Streisand — "California's Pot Clubs May Go Up in Smoke," *U.S. News & World Report*, March 30, 1998.

Stacie Stukin — "Rx Marijuana," *POZ*, December 1997. Available from LLC, 349 W. Twelfth St., New York, NY 10014-1721.

Andrew Peyton Thomas — "Marijuana and Mea Culpas," *American Enterprise*, May/June 1997.

Arnold Trebach and Joseph A. Califano Jr. — "Medical Marijuana." *World & I*, March 1997. Available from 3600 New York Ave. NE, Washington, DC 20002.

Ingrid Wickelgren — "Marijuana: Harder Than Thought?" *Science*, June 27, 1997.

Index